# mentoring

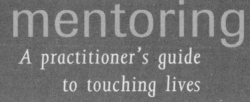

# mentoring
*A practitioner's guide*
*to touching lives*

SUNIL UNNY GUPTAN

**Response Books**
A division of SAGE Publications
New Delhi / Thousand Oaks / London

First published in 2006 by

**Response Books**
A division of Sage Publications India Pvt Ltd
B-42, Panchsheel Enclave
New Delhi 110 017

**Sage Publications Inc**          **Sage Publications Ltd**
2455 Teller Road          1 Oliver's Yard, 55 City Road
Thousand Oaks, California 91320          London EC1Y 1SP

Published by Tejeshwar Singh for Response Books, phototypeset in
11/13.5 pt Joanna MT by Star Compugraphics Pvt Ltd, Delhi, and printed
at Chaman Enterprises, New Delhi.

**Library of Congress Cataloging-in-Publication Data**

Guptan, Sunil Unny
    Mentoring: a practitioner's guide to touching lives/Sunil Unny
Guptan.
        p. cm.
    Includes index.
    1. Mentoring in business—Handbooks, manuals, etc.   2. Mentoring
in the professions—Handbooks, manuals, etc.   I. Title.

HF5385.G76      658.3'124—dc22      2006      2006027768

**ISBN:** 10: 0–7619–3528–2 (PB)      10: 81–7829–683–7 (India–PB)
        13: 978–0–7619–3528–5 (PB)   13: 978–81–7829–683–8 (India–PB)

**Production Team:** Vidyadhar Gadgil, Rajib Chatterjee and
                    Santosh Rawat

To
My father,
UNNY
The greatness of the man lies in
not making any pretensions to it

# contents

# Contents

# preface

GETTING ahead in life would have been an easy business if each of us had had a liberal dose of luck and foresight, and wisdom beyond our years. While luck is as unpredictable a commodity as they come, foresight and wisdom have been on offer through the years for all who have sought them in the right places. Foresight and wisdom come with age, and those who have gone ahead of us have an ample supply—more than they might need for themselves. These they offer to the people following after them. While some, as mentors, offer them on a platter for free, others put a price on them.

Mentors are not a new kind of person in this world. They have long been around, touching lives and practicing their magical craft, making wonders out of ordinary people—and all for free. This has been an informal arrangement for eons, and a pretty successful one at that. All through history, in all civilizations and cultures, mentors have left their visible mark.

The modern-day organization, in its quest for greater efficiency and maximization of resource value, has co-opted mentoring into its repertoire of learning and development interventions. The result has been the systematization and organization of an ancient practice to suit modern require-ments. Formality, clarity of roles, approach, codification of relationship content and measurement of output have been added by modern organizations to an old practice.

Not all aspects of the ancient practice fit; those that don't have been excised, while those that are advantageous have been accentuated.

Just as organizations outside India have their own brand of mentors working within their cultural context, Indian organizations have theirs, with subtle differences born out of the Indian cultural and historical experience with *Gurus* and mentors. Although in India the practice is much older, it is a lot less recognized within Indian organizations.

Encouraging mentoring and setting up mentoring schemes are practices that have been catching on in Indian organizations in recent years. Quite a few practices, though not mentoring as such, are being passed off under the appellation of mentoring. It is good when they work out well, but when they don't, it is mentoring as a process that is left carrying the blame.

I have worked in this area for about a decade, training mentors, helping design and implement mentoring schemes, and performing a hand-holding function for organizations for a period of time during the interventions. It is certainly most satisfying to see the idea of mentoring take root and flourish in organizations and the social set-up.

Quite a few organizations have contributed to building this pool of experience in setting up mentoring schemes, and also in using external mentors to help in the learning and development process. I would like to acknowledge two organizations in particular for adding to my learning, experience, and wisdom in bringing out this work: the National Thermal Power Corporation (NTPC) and Dr. Reddy's Laboratories (DRL).

Mr. A.N. Dave, Mr. Ashok Swarup, Mr. Nagakumar, and so many other executives of NTPC have been a valuable resource for so much of my experience in helping set up a comprehensive mentoring system in a large organization, encompassing several units geographically spread across the length and breadth of India. Starting from scratch in 2000, NTPC has over the last few years built a credible pool of qualified and practicing mentors, numbering almost 250, covering almost all their far-flung units. Many in the lower echelons of the organization have also worked hard to make this happen. Mr. Jayant Kumar, Mr. John Phillip, Ms. Debsmita Panda, and Ms. Kanchana Shahi Gupta impressed me with their commitment to the cause and their work in helping mentoring take root in the outlying units of NTPC.

Mr. Rakesh Sharma, as head of HR in the old DRL, had invited me to be a part of a planned change process eight years ago. I am glad I accepted and stayed to see an organization morph from a small family-run company into a giant Indian MNC. Mr. Atul Davle, now more of a friend, had a few years ago gone through the organization-sponsored Executive Coaching (and External Mentor) intervention at DRL. He has been an active votary of spreading the benefits of the process to the top executives in DRL. Now, the lead taken by Mr. G.V. Prasad in executive coaching and mentoring has borne fruit and the program is doing very well.

This book is intended to help both those already in the practice of mentoring and those just wading in now. It is a walk-through of what mentoring is and what can be expected from it for the practitioner and the recipient. As a user guide and as a manual for the novice, the book is designed as a route map to the magical journey of mentoring.

This book is intended to be a source of information and resources, revealing what mentoring, behind its cloak of myth and mystery, really is and is not and what the mentoring process is all about, offering a window into the mind of the mentor, understanding the competencies and skills required of a mentor, clarifying issues in mentoring, and describing how to set up a mentoring scheme in an organization.

The case studies and mini case studies are of actual events and people experiencing mentoring. The liberty taken in writing a case, cutting through the clutter of redundant information to highlight certain issues, is unavoidable. Names and places have been altered out of respect for the confidentiality involved in the mentoring process. The writing style in the cases also uses fictional techniques to enhance readability.

In the making of this work, I have my friend Leela Kirloskar of Response Books to thank. If not for her persistent reminders and the enthusiasm she infused in me to pick up the pace of work in writing, this book would certainly have been delayed much longer because of my preoccupations with work, teaching assignments and family.

There are also many people who have been a part of this work, contributing to the wisdom and learning written about here. They have supported me throughout my personal journey and my gratitude to them all can hardly be expressed in words. Mentoring is about touching lives and helping to transform them. This has been my journey.

# a personal journey

FIVE days into July, 27 years ago, as yet a teenager, I stood in helpless silence at the foot of the hospital bed, gently stroking the soft feet I held in my hands. At the other end of the bed, the army doctor struggled with the cardiac massage, and then the one-final-try injection to jump-start the heart that had in the end given up. The good doctor finally straightened up, looked at my mother, then glanced at me, and slowly shook his head.

It was only as the years passed that I began to gradually come to terms with the void left behind—the absence of someone to match wits with, to trust more than you might yourself, the certainty that the reassuring presence would always be there, the feeling of a safety net person that enables you to leap higher and farther, the one who believes in you and gets you to believe in yourself ... I still miss him so.

He had been the one person who took the trouble to study me to find the hidden energies and resources within. He had the ability to see beyond what was visible to the ordinary eye. I could believe in him, for he believed in me. Not just because he was my father, but because he was that kind of man.

In his little-known village, way beyond the reach of urban facilities, he was an icon and an inspiration for the next couple of generations of relatives and ordinary village folk. He had dared to venture to enlist in the army when few would have sought any form of work beyond walkable distance from the village. When he returned on his annual leave almost every year, I saw the respect and near-veneration that people held him in. Many people of the succeeding generation had followed him in breaking out of the narrow confines of social and familial comfort. He had been an icon and inspiration for them.

Simplicity and an unpretentious demeanor had been his hallmark. Soft-spoken and patient, he had held himself, through bad times and good, with the dignity that his generation had held dear. This he carried with him to the very end. Giving without counting the cost, helping when help could be given in whatever form, taking that intimate and personal interest in all who sought him out in search of help, not holding back from many to prevent a few taking undue advantage of his largesse—these were his sterling qualities. Not that he had any material wealth to speak of, but he had a sagacity and wisdom that went far beyond the measurable. These he effectively used to lead many from being very ordinary to becoming something more.

He was more to me than just a father. He was the inspiration of a simple outlook: when you can, do help someone in need. Today, to the bane and discomfort of a few who love me dearly, I have inherited this belief and perhaps practice it to an uncomfortable degree. But then his influence has, I believe, been so strong that I owe him so much of whatever I have made of myself and the direction I find myself going in.

To me, he has been my first and greatest mentor.

Life has been good to me in this respect. I have had people travel with me in life who have shown me the path when I dithered in doubt. My faith in mentors, I have always believed, has sent me mentors who have contributed substantially towards sculpting my professional growth and maturation, and also the founding of my personal philosophy of life.

Having splendid heads of institutions that I have studied in, and a succession of very inspiring teachers, have been my greatest fortune. They have been the reason behind my taking the directions I did, and cultivating and retaining the wide variety of interests I have today. The crucial difference has been that these people believed in me and gave me the confidence to believe in myself.

In my high school days, Mrs. Rajeshwari (Victor) gave me that little nudge needed to make me strive to be above the ordinary. Professor A.P. Rajaratnam, my beloved school principal, who taught me to love the language and whose legacy I still carry with me, and Mr. William J. Lazarus, the school correspondent and administrator, were larger-than-life at that time. Now I see that the greatness in them was that they were able to see extraordinary talent in young boys and girls and get them to develop and realize their potential rather than sink back into the comfort of the commonplace. In their small way and in that small place they were great mentors.

Another towering principal, this time in college, took me under his wing and showed me the infinite possibilities in thinking beyond the narrow confines of the immediate. There are many people who would gratefully vouch for the difference Mr. C. Sudarsan made in their lives. The path he lit up helped so many travel much farther than they would have otherwise. I owe to him the maturity and the strength of honesty and integrity that I developed under his guidance.

In my professional life I have had the unique opportunity to ride on the shoulders of two giants. To them I owe much of my professional capability today.

Professor E.G. Parameswaran of Osmania University passed away last year. In his passing, generations of students from many disciplines, not only in Osmania University but also in other institutions, mourned the loss of a mentor in every sense of the word. Professor Parameswaran touched several lives, and those that he touched were transformed in so many ways.

There have been the most rebellious and cantankerous of students, those whom the university system had given up on and was just waiting to be rid of. There have been the most intellectual and brilliant students, those who would have been the best no matter where they chose to be. There have been very ordinary and average students, those who would never have been missed or noticed otherwise. But the touch of Professor Parameswaran transformed them into works of magic, excelling in what they had taken up. They have today made themselves into leading citizens in different walks of life in different parts of the world. Professor Parameswaran, the gentle psychology professor, a renowned scholar in his own right, had not only the rare ability to spot good minds but also the courage to back them in creating the exceptional out of what would otherwise be very ordinary.

It was Professor Parameswaran who encouraged me to return to Osmania University to teach, rather than continuing as an active journalist—the career for which I had trained. Some of my most tumultuous experiences at Osmania I negotiated under his guidance and with his silent support. My leaving Osmania for the Administrative Staff College of India (ASCI) was also at his urging. In hindsight, that too had been a landmark decision for me. The timing and the feel for the kind of assignment that would suit me could only have come from someone with a deep insight into the person I was. In the coming years, I had the good fortune of completing my Ph.D. under his guidance.

Professor Parameswaran had not just been a guide and teacher to me; he was also my mentor and intellectual guardian. I could not have asked for anybody better. I miss him and deeply mourn his passing, not just for myself but for all those who no longer have such a person in their lives.

ASCI is where I came into my own in my professional life. There is a certain ring of coincidence in the succession of good opportunities that has come my way. At ASCI I came to work with Professor B.R. Virmani. He is one of the finest professionals in Human Resource Training and Development in this part of the world. And he practiced what he had taught in his training sessions: that people development is an integral part of any manager's responsibility.

Looking back, I realize that I must have been a rudderless young man with the impatient energy to make things happen—happen yesterday if that were possible. Working closely with Professor Virmani for over a decade nurtured in me the patience and the ability to channel my energies in the right direction. He encouraged me to work independently to create a niche for myself in a competitive but nurturing and supportive environment. This was how I found the confidence to step out and stand on my own feet in later years.

Professor Virmani has been the Guru who opened to me the world of organizations and people development in organizations. From being a journalist by training, practice and teaching, with his support and help I morphed into a professional in training and development, creating my own niche and specialization. As a result, in later years, I have grown to be able to design and direct training interventions for directors of major national and international organizations, chief ministers and state ministers, senior officers in the Indian Administrative Service, Indian Police Service, Indian Foreign Service, and several others.

As a mentor, he has been among the most successful in creating successful professionals and nurturing their growth. The best features of him as a mentor are his firm and tough hand clothed in a comforting and encouraging demeanor, and his clarity of purpose and commitment to the cause he espoused. During the years we worked closely together, I came to admire the way he had handled our professional disagreements and differences. Much of my learning and practice in later years as a mentor has been from the examples and instances I had seen him take people through. My Guru as a people development professional is Professor Balraj Virmani.

It is my good fortune to have had a succession of inspiring people with whom I could chart the course of my progress and growth. People with whom I could sharpen my mind on the grindstone of intellectual debate; who would share unreservedly the wisdom garnered over long years; from whom I could learn and thus not have to reinvent the wheel:

this is the stuff mentors are made of. Great things come in small, innocuous packages.

Such have been the people who have also inspired me to strive and to emulate their deeds. In a quaint, more than half-a-century-old bookshop in the bustling heart of Secunderabad sits a 78-year-old bookseller, Ramakrishna Narsing Acharya. Almost all his life, Mr. Acharya has lived amidst books. They have been his passion and his reason for being. As a business, the bookshop would long ago have gone under in the numerous tumults that Mr. Acharya had weathered. For him it is not a business but a passion to be among books. He has also seen three or four generations of readers come by and sip at the silent intellectual oasis that has been his bookshop.

I have been among those who have grown up in this way. I also saw my schoolteachers go to this bookshop. Mr. Acharya was then a figure of respect and somebody we held in awe for the enormous information and knowledge he had on books we had barely heard of. He always helped those in need of help. I often heard of him simply gifting books to people who could not afford to buy them, or to their children so that they could read and grow. Mr. Acharya has been a guide and mentor to generations of young people who have come to him to seek guidance and direction in their careers and lives. Decades later people have dropped in at the shop, if only to participate in his tireless passion and express a word of gratitude for having helped them become what they are today.

It is only a coincidence that years later he became a part of my extended family and I could get a more intimate look at the working of his passion—his interest in helping and contributing to the larger cause of developing the community he is part of. The tireless energy that he exudes, the enthusiasm that spurs him to travel across the city twice each day, commuting between home and the shop at the age of 78, the sparkle in his eye when he enters his beloved shop—I have always hoped to have at least some of this when I get to be his age. As an inspiration, it is hard to find a more revered icon.

There must certainly be something in the sights and experiences of early days that shapes one's thinking and philosophy. Within me, I do bear the evidence of the influence of seeing so often the devoted care of the sick and the injured, of the loyalty and commitment that only an army nurse is capable of. Kamala spent an entire career in the Military Nursing Service of the Indian Army in Secunderabad. I recall well the sights I saw as a child, of her duty and work in different wards of the hospital. Retired from the service a decade ago, Kamala, my mother, is still a source of strength.

During the years that I have myself grown to be a mentor to people, I have learned much from those who have grown with my support and guidance. The benefits of reverse mentoring are immense when one is open to the humility of learning from all who can teach, whatever their age or station in life.

The person from whom I have learnt the most in this form is my companion, my friend, my co-traveller for the past decade and a half: my wife Surekha. So much versatility, so much talent, so much creativity packed into one person can only lead to quite a bit of it rubbing off on those who spend time with her. Over the years I have been witness and participant as she had a variety of successful careers, and as her personality matured. From top copywriter, to creative consultant, to technical writer, to Web designer, to feng shui consultant, to family and parenting counselor, she has not only reveled in all roles but also risen to the pinnacle of each one. In addition, there is the vast reservoir of talent not used professionally: music, painting, needlework, interior decoration....

Her successes have been as delightful to watch as they have been a pride to be a part of. In small but sure steps she has overcome several turbulences and uncertainties, each more challenging than the other. As she emerged from each she was that much stronger. Strength and determination, steadfastness and faith are qualities I have learnt in large measure from her.

And then, there is this little girl, Ishitaa, who has been elected as the role model for the students in her school in classes following hers. The innocence that lets honesty be valued higher than duplicity, integrity higher than quick-fix solutions, and natural charm higher than cultivated niceness are some of the things I have learnt from her and passed on to other people, many years older than her but still running short in these qualities. I am proud of my daughter and in all humility acknowledge so much that I have learnt from her.

Quite a few people have contributed in no small measure to this effort. They have been a part of my journey through life and have afforded me the opportunity to learn from them. In recent years, as I moved to work with individualized learning, and executive coaching and mentoring, I have had greater insights into people and the complex nature of their concerns.

Some have stayed with me over the years and now we share friendship rather than just a professional relationship.

Two dear friends and former colleagues from my years in ASCI—Professors Umeshwar Pandey and Muralidharan—have been valuable to me in the past and are as valuable even today. They have been my close friends and have taught me different ways of handling people—from work-men and trade union leaders to CEOs and ministers—in a wide spectrum and range of situations.

Many individuals have also been a part of my dream of aiding those in need. They have, in their own ways, become a part of me and my life. In number they may be far too many to list, but I acknowledge with gratitude their role in shaping me and my thinking.

Dr. P.G. Koshy has, as a peer, been a vital part of my growing years and for over three decades has provided a friendship that has been my benchmark for the triumph of trust over triviality and mutual respect over differences in outlook. To me there has never been a better example of a person who can survive adversities piled on beyond endur-ance and still stand triumphant. In my worst moments of weakness or defeat, Koshy has been a source of strength—helping me to see that if he can still be standing in the face of all that he has been through, I have no right to complain.

For someone who calls himself a first-generation literate, Dr. Sravan Kumar is a remarkable example of how persever-ance and hard work can overcome any obstacle. A young man and a very fine mind, he took his first job in one of my projects, and I have learnt so much from him. The humility to acknowledge ignorance and a willingness to learn, and not letting one's ego stand in the way of any learning op-portunity have been the qualities that have brought him so much success. From where he started to where he is now is a testament to the fact that no excuse can be valid if you have the desire and the humility to learn.

Ms. Vidya Mani has afforded me an opportunity to take a close look at the complex workings of a highly intelligent and sharp young mind. She has been of great help to me in understanding the concerns and character of the youth of today and in getting the measure of the courage it takes to be steadfast in the face of adversity and ill fortune. She has been a part of this work, helping to clarify a few of the contentious issues here.

Aruna Gopalakrishnan, Dr. P. Geetha, Vijay Pratap, Pankaj Kumar, and Sindhu Shanmugam have in their unique ways aided me in getting a perspective on how each generation experiences mentoring differently.

All these people have been a part of this personal journey. I expect that many more will join me in this endeavor and perhaps contribute to my becoming that much wiser. I am grateful to each for giving me what they did. I shall stay steadfast to my commitment to continue touching lives, and hope that in some form many more will be the beneficiaries of the joy and delight I have had in redistributing learning and wisdom.

# WHO SHOULD READ THIS BOOK

WHAT's in this book for a practitioner? Why should she/he be investing time and energy into reading what she/he is already doing? Fair enough that these questions should be asked at the start itself....

There may be several small checks and cautions that have been bypassed unknowingly or without our realizing that they may be subtle but still important. Here is a run-through of the checks and cautions for those who are already practicing mentors, whether in their personal space or in organizations....

## CHECKS AND CAUTIONS FOR THE PRACTITIONER

### 1. Check-list of what to do

There are quite a few of us who come into practicing an activity more by chance than design. Many of us are quite some way down the road before we pause and look back at the road we have traveled and try to see whether this was the best course, or whether there were better ways of traveling the same route. Would there be more efficient ways, without the boulders we had to skirt around, without the larger stones we stumbled over, or the small sharp pebbles that had hurt our feet. Surely there would be better ways that are less troublesome?

People such as these are ones that may like to look at the route map in the mentoring process and the guiding tips to adding that much more to the joy of being involved in it and getting it done better.

And then there are those of us who have ventured in after systematic study and initiation. This is a series of check-lists in the practice of mentoring in organizations and in the personal domain. They are valuable inputs to constantly check the direction we are moving in and ensure that the path is taking us in the direction we intend to go.

In either case, there are lists and steps that lead the practicing mentors in a course of introspection and a mid-course inventory of practices. And for those a little fuzzy about the way forward, there are suggestive steps and actions that some who have traveled this road before have found successful.

## 2. Different perspectives on what to do

In considering the course of action in a given circumstance, the best would be to have an understanding of all or most of the different ways of action. This makes the choice a considered one rather than a speculative one. Also there is far less dependence on luck and favorable environmental conditions when the data is available to make an informed choice. This is one major consideration in the crucial nature and value attached to the practice of mentoring itself.

Further, the considerations and the practices listed here are those encountered in an environment that is character-istically Indian. The cultural subtleties that pervade Indian organizations make it essential that the documented practices and their systematic renditions be customized before considering implementation.

Different perspectives and opinions, practices and experiences add much to the understanding of the practitioner in sharpening her/his approach to mentoring. There is also the chance of adding novel and innovative approaches to the practices already in place.

## 3. A confirmation of direction

Ever so often, it is always good on any journey to take a periodic check to see if we are still moving in the right direction and along the right path. This is so even if we have been down the road many times over. When dealing with people who are evolving and changing constantly, where the dynamics and characteristics are morphing continuously, this becomes all the more necessary. This is an opportunity to look at the route that others are traveling, to check our own, and confirm that the directions have not unwittingly shifted without our being conscious of it.

The practices in mentoring are strewn with several small curves and hidden pathways, shadowy and misty areas. Even the more experienced traveler on this road is at times a bit unsure about the correctness of what is being done. Rather than base judgment only on instinct, it would augur well to check with practices and experiences of other practitioners as well.

## 4. Confirm what is being done

Reassurance is always comforting. There are times—and this could happen to the best of us—when even the things we have done so many times over seem not so correct. There are times when even the most confident of us needs that little bit of hand-holding and the warmth of reassurance. This works wonders for our confidence and our commitment to the cause we are dedicated to.

In mentoring there is sometimes a feeling of isolation in terms of not being able to check with others the specifics of the practices and paths chosen. There is the comfort of getting to know if the choices are correct without compromising the commitments made. To the practitioner, the compilation of experiences and a systematic narrative of the steps and discussions on issues serve well to confirm the correctness of what is being done or make corrections where necessary and possible.

## 5.  Try another approach

Being limited by one's own thinking, being a captive of one's own experience, or sticking to the approaches often tried is many times a virtue. But there comes a time when the need is to be able to work at newer approaches, to mutate deliberately into variations that can be more effective in practice.

It certainly helps to know others' experimentations and experiences to configure one's own approach to experimentation, or for that matter to seek another method or activity that could yield better results. Building knowledge about the variety of approaches and thus expanding one's own repertoire is an asset in mentoring.

## 6.  Expand horizons

Having a wide intellectual horizon is a certain asset to a mentor. The wide and varied perspective that one is able to bring to the process adds so much value to the mentee and to the process itself. That makes the mentor an invaluable asset herself/himself. Understanding the process and the different ways it can be viewed and experienced is in itself a sure way of widening personal horizons.

The more the mentor is in the know of things regarding the process, the better equipped she/he will be. This helps in traveling beyond one's own experience. And participating in others' experiences pushes the limits of one's own perspectives further out. Sharing and then ruminating on the experience and thoughts of others; understanding the process from different points of view; and also a systematic reading of the nuances involved in the practice makes for reaching out beyond the thresholds of one's own limitations.

## 7. Enlarge the repertoire of capabilities, perspectives, and skills

What better can a mentee ask for than to be working with a mentor having an expansive range of capability and skills, and with an understanding of the different views, perspectives and opinions on the issues at hand?

The continuing endeavor of the mentor should be not only to understand the different competencies and skills involved but also the means of improving on them. There are also quite a few skills and capabilities that would be lying dormant or unused, the mentor being unaware of their existence. This is a good opportunity to refresh the window of personal skill and competency resources and see new ones emerge. There are enormous benefits from working to better oneself constantly and trying every opportunity.

## 8. Systematic and organized approach

Oftentimes, the difficulty for most practitioners is to get the process and the steps to be taken organized, documented and systematically explained so that the practice goes well and smoothly. This task—to put them all in perspective and conceptualize them in models to be followed so that the path is cleared and well explained—is often left to the academics.

The understanding of the practice of mentoring; the steps in the process; the skills and competencies and their applications; the issues that could surface and how one needs to handle them; all these when presented in a systematic and organized manner add so much to the value of the mentor's functioning.

## 9. Reaffirm faith in mentoring

There is nobility in the practice of mentoring. But then, like all noble activities and intentions, there is also the downside of setbacks and derision. This is one of the main causes of the flagging of the faith of those engaged in mentoring.

In reading and getting in touch with the experiences of others, in understanding the calling better, in taking a refresher course in the activity, and in the celebration of success in mentoring with others, there is always a renewal of faith and the will to carry on. One of the objectives of this book is to offer these to the practitioner.

## 10. Seek new energy

From the renewal of faith comes the feeling of being refreshed and the energy to go forth again and push the limits. The practicing mentor can seek a booster and a shot of energy from getting a look at others in the same or similar pursuit and commitment. The energy one exudes in this line of work not only rejuvenates the mentee but also the spirits of other mentors.

This is one of the principal reasons why organizations often encourage mentors to get together and share their experiences, concerns and their successes, and overcome travails in the process of mentoring. Without compromising the commitment of confidentiality to the mentee and the process, the mentors can seek new energies from each other not only in trying out newer approaches and paths but also from the celebration of each other's successes. In this respect, documentation serves as a sort of energy concentrate.

## 11. Find new meaning to work and help

Mentors are always very altruistic people, and that is basic to them. There is so much to what they do that does not go by the usual tenets that govern others. Their fulfillment goes beyond the expectation of tangible rewards for their effort. That is one of the prime reasons they are respected and often revered.

They find ineffable warmth and meaning in what they do ... and in the activity of each of them is a subtly different kind of meaning. In reading up on the different viewpoints on the subject, they could find altogether different meanings and perspectives on what they feel about what they do. This is something any practitioner could look forward to.

This could also provide them new energy to take their special work forward and, in a sense, discover new ways and means to add significance and value to mentoring.

## 12. Enjoy the intangible fruits more

The mentor does not count the fruits on the tree she/he nurtures. She/he does not even expect to be handed any benefits for what she/he has helped create. The fruits are intangible and something that only the mentor can herself/himself can feel and experience. The joy of these is infinite and there are no limits to the bliss in being the recipient. All one needs to do to understand this is to ask any mentor....

Mentors can find greater joy and delight in finding newer ways to work further in this mission. This intangible fruit would taste even better in many ways and help the practicing mentor to share in the joys of other mentors.

## 13. Greater pay-off for the mentees

Adding value to the mentor is adding value to the mentee. The benefits of greater awareness and understanding in the mentor will definitely, in some form or the other, be passed on to the mentee. The work here—creating this advisory and compilation for the better practice of mentoring—also has that intent in mind.

## CAUTIONS FOR THE MENTOR

Having talked about the advantages, this book for the practitioner is also a walk-through of some of the cautions that the mentor must heed. It also serves to help the mentor not to get into situations that she/he should avoid finding herself/himself in. Some of the help that the mentor reading this may get is described below.

## 1. Avoiding unknown pitfalls during the course of mentoring

There are scores of sticky ends and tricky situations that the mentor might find herself/himself in during the process. Quite a few of them would have come up earlier by now or would have been pre-empted in thought. However, there are always situations and demands placed on the mentor that may not be foreseen by the mentor herself/himself. These are the situations that could cause the mentor to encounter a major crisis.

These pitfalls are the knotty ones in the process. The known and the foreseen are easier to handle but those unknown to the mentor are problematic. This book gives the mentor a wide array of experiences and practices encountered during the process, and anticipates many that are common as well as some that are tricky. Bringing them to the fore helps the practitioner to avoid tripping on the stone others may have already stumbled over.

## 2. Knowing more of the mentee's expectations

The experience of training mentors and mentees lends the advantage of knowing first-hand the different expectations that they carry into the process. The wide array of expectations that the mentees—young and old, freshers and experienced—have of the mentor, the processes involved and the organizations that might be sponsoring the scheme are covered here.

The practicing mentor may have encountered some or many of them. Understanding the subtle and explicit expectations of mentees in different settings will be an invaluable help in dealing with them more effectively. Further, it does go a long way towards providing for the possibilities of taking on a variety of mentees in future. This adds much value to the experience of the mentor too.

## 3. Avoiding unpleasant possibilities

Introducing the practitioner to possibilities that lurk just around the next corner could be of so much help in not stumbling into one of them. This book contains cautions and detailing of the steps that need to be taken in ensuring that such unpleasant results do not befall an unwary yet earnest traveler on this august path of mentoring.

Such a satisfying experience of being involved in the development and growth of someone else should not be marred by any hint of unpleasantness. However the ideal is not always the norm. It is therefore always prudent to be cautious in this venture. This book also intends to take the experienced practitioner through the well-worn paths as well as the less-traveled ones, so as to serve as cautions to them against the possibility of unpleasant experiences and to pre-empt undesired outcomes in the process.

## 4. Not getting mired in organizational or system dynamics

The system—be it the organization or the social environment —is an ever-present entity. There is no wishing it away. It is best to understand it and roll with the waves as it sweeps past.

The mentor has to contend with this entity in its various *avatars*. There are always the undercurrents and dynamics within the system. Cautioning the practitioner about this helps in terms of not getting entangled with the unpleasant aspects of the dynamics and getting mired in the unproductive events. The systematic approach to understanding how the mentoring scheme can be introduced in the organization and how the mentors should be afforded the liberty to operate unfettered within the ethics and the norms of mentoring would help in easing the pains of anyone stung by the wrong end of it.

More important is being forewarned, which keeps one wary of the seamy dynamics that snares the unwary. Being aware is being forearmed to avoid and stay clear of the unwanted entanglements—not just for the mentors but also the mentees, who need to be warned of the calamities that might befall them if they are not careful.

## 5. Stop from being hustled into situations

With the best of intentions, the mentor may not be as cautious and wary as might be necessary for the kind of mentees and organizational keepers that she/he may have to face. Faith is not always an appreciated virtue ... at times it does become a needless liability. That is when the problem strikes.

The mentor may out of the goodness of her/his heart agree to do things that she/he is not quite aware of the import of. There is also the possibility of being talked into situations that she/he may not want to be a part of. This is more to do with the mentor not being conscious or aware of the different ways in which the system and people operate. Not that mentors are gullible people, but being cautious is better than being hustled into something one may not even know about.

This book also adds to the general awareness of the different kinds of practices that pervade the organization and the social system under the guise of mentoring.

## 6. Wide range of cautions for the practitioner

The book also offers a range of cautions, both direct and in the form of experiences of people who have ventured earlier into mentoring. The cautions in some cases are mentioned as direct advice and in other places in the form of case studies documenting live experiences.

## FOR THE ADMINISTRATORS, COORDINATORS, AND CHAMPIONS OF THE MENTORING SCHEME

In these, the practicing mentor can find value in strengthening her/his understanding of the process and the forms the practice can take. It is for the mentor to make the best of the documentation and the indicators in the experiences and compilations here.

| Case study 1.1 | Home away from home |
|---|---|

The organization had prospered well in the past. For over a quarter of a century, since it acquired an independent identity, it has been expanding all around. Sound financial performance year after year, phenomenal growth in size and spread, a substantial pool of qualified workers in the sector, and a host of other indicators had given the organization a strong positive self-image. The organization had now grown to being the pride of the sector.

CONTINUED ON THE NEXT PAGE

CASE STUDY 1.1—CONTINUED

The organization had prided itself on having the ability to attract highly qualified and intelligent young people from established and reputed engineering institutions. This had for long been its pride. That the young and fresh engineers should have a good and pleasant work environment, even if away from their homes and in remote areas, was a belief that the top management had lived with for many years.

This background made the shock even more severe when it hit. The top team could not digest it when it hit them. 'It is not possible,' they had said initially, 'there must be something else causing this.' They even refused to use the word 'problem.'

Two young trainee engineers in different locations far apart had committed suicide that particular year and six others had quit within a few weeks of joining. The seriousness of the matter shook the top management enough to look critically at the events in the lives of the young graduate engineers when they joined the organization and were posted in different locations.

It certainly was a 'problem,' they finally admitted, leading them to take measures of planning specific interventions to address the issue in future. The location, the nature of jobs and the living conditions could not be faulted. The need was to give them a human face to associate with rather than an officious organizational hand administering the process of integration. The feeling side of the organization, which had been long buried in the pursuit of success, had to be resurrected. There could be no quick-fix solution, no one-step answers, but only systematic and meticulous work to get the young to feel wanted and at home away from home.

The buddy system and mentoring came into being a part of the organizational culture over the next few years.

Benefits for the 'organization people'

1. Different perspectives and experiences
2. Better understanding of the mentor and the mentee
3. Clarity in understanding the process
4. Check-list for missed steps in the process
5. Make approach more systematic
6. Check organization and organizational culture readiness for the scheme
7. Getting top management buy-in
8. Guide map for introducing the scheme
9. Getting better design for training of mentors
10. Preventive maintenance
11. Make any adaptive changes to make it more effective
12. Tips on cautions
13. Tips on signs and symptoms to look for
14. Diagnosis of any malady before it becomes serious
15. Cautions in measurement and evaluation
16. Setting realistic expectations
17. Pre-empt and prevent exploitation of the scheme

There are quite a few organizations in India that have ventured into introducing mentoring as a people development activity. Many have introduced it in name with the actual practice being something quite different. (This happens more out of not knowing specifically what the scheme and the process entail than out of deliberate bad intent.)

The sponsors and the champions of the scheme in organizations have much to gain from the documentation here. There are a number of lessons that those in organizations—

both those setting themselves the responsibility of introducing such a scheme or those being asked to maintain the scheme in organizations—can garner from this book.

How other organizations have experienced the scheme and what their gains have been is one of the crucial inputs into considering such an intervention in one's own organization. There may be a lot of similarities between our own organization and the organization that has taken up the scheme. This itself is a good reason to explore what has been their experience in this direction.

Getting a better understanding of the current group of mentors and mentees (and prospective ones) contributes to making the scheme more successful. This understanding would be of a great help to the mentoring champion, sponsor or coordinator of the scheme in working out the cost (not just monetary) and the benefits that accrue to the organization in taking up this intervention.

There is also a great need for the coordinator in the organization to have an intimate knowledge of the working of the mentoring process, especially in the Indian environment. This is essential in selling the scheme internally and showcasing the efficiency and effectiveness of it to ensure involvement in it. Further, it is a great way to get a top management buy-in into the scheme by explaining its benefits in as much detail as possible. The good understanding of the working of the process will also enable the coordinator to troubleshoot any routine hitches that may arise in the course of running the developmental scheme.

The introduction of the mentoring scheme as a developmental initiative requires a systematic approach for it to run smoothly. It is also essential that the scheme be introduced and run in specific sequential steps, so as to not only ensure success but also enable those involved in it to adapt. There is always the chance of inadvertent missed steps that become stumbling blocks. Being familiar with the sequence and the rationale of the process helps coordinators in organizations to keep a check on it.

Having a structure and an advisory contributes much to making the approach that much more methodical and systematic. This is also important for those following the working of the scheme, as it enables them to plug into it without unnecessary dependence on the coordinator or the administrator. The success of the coordinator is as much in how smoothly the scheme runs without her/his active intervention as on how much of her/his advice may be followed. The steps suggested here in the mentoring process and also the introduction of the scheme in organizations can contribute to making the approach more meticulous.

Even before the scheme is thought out and introduced, it is very essential to check whether the organization and its culture are ready to accept such interventions. The checklist and diagnostic tool can help decide the course of action in designing and introducing mentoring as a developmental intervention. Further, there is the issue of making sure that the mentors who are at the core of the intervention have a training and developmental input to ensure success.

More important is getting the top management to accept this and buy into the idea itself. Ensuring this support can go a long way in ensuring the longevity and success of the scheme.

For the organization and the coordinator of the scheme, this book could also serve as a manual or guidebook for performing a preventive maintenance on the scheme to ensure continued good health. Like the moving parts of any functioning machinery, the mentoring scheme too has a need for continual care and maintenance. The good strategy of any mechanic is also very much applicable here: to carry out periodic preventive maintenance. The advisory in the book is a good check-list to carry this process through.

Constant nurturing and care also affords the opportunity to make any necessary adaptive changes to make the system and the scheme more efficient and productive. Further, tips on cautions to be taken also reduce the chances of falling into any difficulty during the run-time of the scheme. These are cautions not just for the administrator and coordinator of the scheme, but also for the practicing mentors and mentees in the organization.

Like any living organism, the mentoring scheme too has maladies that can afflict it from the inside. As such the recognition of something not going all too well can only be obtained from the signs and symptoms that surface. Capturing these and reading the symptoms is crucial in diagnosing the malady that has visited the scheme or parts of it. The lists and the narration of experiences here provide the reader a good indicator of the signs and symptoms to look out for. It also provides indicators on how a coordinator or the mentoring champion in organizations can diagnose measures going wrong in the scheme.

One of the touchiest parts of the scheme is the measurement of, and criteria for success of the scheme. This also involves some form of the indications of success of mentors in the organization. These are areas that we must tread on with caution and care. Tips in this regard are valuable lessons for the mentoring champion and the coordinators of the scheme in the organization.

Guarding against misusing the fair name of the process and the hard-earned reputation of the scheme is something that the organization must do. Misuse is a distinct possibility in an organization fraught with internecine dynamics and game playing. Being watchful and cautious is a prudent measure. The indications of misuse and manipulation give the coordinator and administrator a warning to sound alarm bells to halt its spread.

Such are the benefits to be had from this book for the administrator, coordinator, and champion of the mentoring scheme in organizations. Be it any form of organization, getting to the spirit and clarity of the role of the mentor is a definite must for its success. The take-away from here is as valuable for the organization and it functionaries, as it is for the practicing mentors and prospective mentees.

## USER GUIDE FOR NEW ENTRANTS TO MENTORING

There are many of us who have the potential, the energy and the zeal to walk down this path, but have for some reason not ventured so far. There is also an uncertainty involved when it is the first time we are venturing into something, which tends to hold one back. Here is a sort of a user guide for those faced with this difficulty. This book helps the new entrant in various ways:

1. Understanding the mentor's role
2. Where to start
3. Understanding the process
4. Signposts on the path ahead

5. Clarifying WIIFM (What's In It For Me)
6. Getting a measure of the competencies and skills required
7. Giving a structure to a random understanding
8. Revealing the hidden corners
9. Lighting up the gray areas
10. Avoiding errors on start-up
11. Understanding the mentees' and the organization's expectations
12. Help in getting the right mentee
13. Getting an idea of others experiences

'Mentor' is a word most of us would have heard many times over. But when we come to asking ourselves specifically what it means and what the mentor actually does, most of us are quite fuzzy about the specifics. Being fuzzy may be okay if one has to just talk about it or discuss the matter in generalities. But it is different when one has to actually play the role of a mentor. The really difficult part is taking on the responsibility for the mentee that goes with the role.

Therefore, before venturing into the deeper side of the practice, it would be prudent to check the waters in understanding the role of the mentor and the working of the process. This also gives the beginner a good idea of where to start and what is best, keeping her/his personality and characteristics in mind. This provides an opportunity to understand the signposts that appear on the journey and to map the route clearly.

Then comes one of the most important aspects of getting into the role of a mentor: getting a fix on WIIFM (What's In It For Me). It is vital that there is clarity on this well before any newcomer wades deeper in. Being unclear lends itself to uncomfortable motives arising in the midst of the process and subverting the development of the relationship. Further it can also lead to irreparable damage to the reputation of the individuals involved as also the image of the mentoring scheme and the intervention. The book helps one to work through this process and get clarity for the beginners in the journey.

Understanding what the race is all about helps the runner be better prepared for the effort. The need is to understand what the skills and competencies required to be an effective and successful mentor are, and also to understand how these can be strengthened if you already have them and, if not, how you can develop them.

The subtle error (which later escalates into a major difficulty) people often make in getting into any developmental activity is to approach it with a random understanding rather than through systematic learning. Giving the approach a specific structure provides not only a protection against possible errors but also an opportunity to keep a check as you proceed of how the process is working. This is invaluable for the new entrant, in terms of making the entry into the mentoring process systematically and with a calculated intent.

This book also helps to give the beginner a preview of the subtle nuances of the process. It also walks the newcomer through the details of the mentoring process that are not immediately obvious to everybody. It also does the necessary hand-holding of the novice in navigating through gray areas and handling delicate issues. The start of any process is crucial, not only in terms of sustaining the interest and energy in it but also in keeping the morale of all involved high. Errors and false starts can make the energy and concern flag. Guarding against this is a lesson to be learnt here.

Getting a preview of the expectations being placed on you as a mentor before you start is definitely an advantage for one beginning her/his venture in mentoring. The lessons in this book are garnered out of experience of dealing with scores of mentors and mentees, a fairly comprehensive knowledge of the expectations that mentees have of mentors, and an understanding of what the organization expects out of the mentor and the mentoring process.

Understanding the mentee—her/his characteristics, outlook, and attitude—helps in terms of getting linked with the right kind of mentee who can suit the mentor best. In reading through the experiences of several mentors, one gets a fairly good view of what the mentee is all about and the cautions one might like to take before choosing a mentee. Others' experience may not necessarily be the kind one might experience oneself, but it is a fair indicator of what is to come.

## EXPECTATION-SETTING FOR THE POTENTIAL MENTEE

Having read through all that mentors can get from this book, the mentees themselves can set their expectations from entering into the mentoring process. Here is an advisory for the mentee on what she/he must keep in mind when venturing into the fold of the mentoring process.

1. Walk in with your eyes open
2. Understand the working of the process

3. Be clear about what one is getting
4. Understand the various expectations
5. Understand how to get the best and the maximum out of the process
6. Get the right mentor
7. Know the mentor's mind
8. Get a check-list on what makes a mentor great
9. Be clear about what to expect from the organization

The book is a contribution to taking mentoring as a developmental intervention forward, not just in an organizational and corporate setting, but also in the personal lives of people. There is much to be gained from mentoring, not only for the mentee but also for the organization and the mentor. A systematic documentation of the experiences and concepts on mentoring is beyond doubt an aid to all involved in the process....

---

**Case study 1.2**    Building the faith in self...

Nobody expected Jose Mathew to make anything of himself. None of his brothers had. The three that were ahead of him in school had barely managed to get past high school, and after that nobody knew what had become of them.

Jose didn't appear very different. If anything, people thought he was the worst of the lot and expected him to follow their path into anonymity. His performance in academics was always poor, and he had difficulty concentrating on his studies. In class he always appeared to lurk around the back benches, and the teachers preferred to ignore him in the overflowing class of over 45 students.

CONTINUED ON THE NEXT PAGE

CASE STUDY 1.2—CONTINUED

He was none too good at sports either. He had a few friends whom he spent time with, not steady enough to be dependable. Everybody found it easy to say that it ran in the family and that he was very much like his brothers.

There was, however, one exception ... Mrs. Akhila Rajeshwar Rao. She taught English in St. Thomas High School where the Mathew brothers studied. There was something about her that endeared her to her students, even the most cantankerous of them. She enjoyed the time she spent with the students and it showed.

'Akhila Ma'am,' as the students called her, saw something that others did not bother to look for. Jose enjoyed music. He dabbled in learning quite a few instruments but did not work steadily with any particular one and this brought him derision from all. But his knowledge of music—the unbelievable knowledge of tunes and songs, the lyrics and singers, the bands and musicians—was, even for a boy in his early teens, phenomenal. He enthusiastically shared this interest and knowledge only with those who showed interest in him.

Akhila Ma'am did, and he spoke to her about his obsession with music and how he spent all his time and even money on it. Akhila spent her time working with Jose in getting past his high school examinations, and in later years following his passion for music in a more systematic and organized manner.

Today all this is a thing of the past for Jose. He is now a VJ and quite popular in most parties and star music festivals in the city and the region. Much sought after by the television and music channels, very successful in his line of work, well paid and much in demand, he has a very comfortable life and lifestyle, and good future to look forward to.

CONTINUED ON THE NEXT PAGE

CASE STUDY 1.2—CONTINUED

'To me what matters is not that I have today all the money that I want and all the material comforts that money can buy, and the world I know is at my feet ... to me what matters is that in those days when I needed it most, only Akhila Ma'am stood by me and believed in me. Only Akhila Ma'am ... not my family ... not my friends ... no-one ... only Akhila Ma'am gave me the courage to dream and achieve what I am today. I meet her every month, but she will not take anything from me ... in my heart, I say a silent prayer for her good health and thank her before every one of my shows,' says Jose Mathew today.

# 2

# GETTING TO KNOW THE MENTOR

## HAVE YOU HAD A MENTOR?

- Was there someone who believed in you even when you doubted yourself?
- Was there someone about whom you find yourself asking 'What would she/he have done?'
- Was there someone who guided you past the fog of confusion and dilemmas and helped you see the path ahead?
- Was there someone who helped you see the hidden strength in yourself?
- Was there someone who helped you chart a course for yourself in life?
- Was there someone who has become an icon for you, someone whom you would like to emulate?
- Was there someone who opened up for you the 'secrets' of her/his own success?

YES, these are people who in their own ways have been torch-bearers for us in times of darkness. If we have had such people in our lives—people who have changed the course of our lives, and made us better people than we would have been otherwise—then we have had mentors. And we have been beneficiaries of mentoring.

## CAN I BE A MENTOR?

Not everybody is a mentor, but anybody can become one. Either you have the attributes, competencies and skills, or—the next best thing—you can develop them. These qualities include:

- Right orientation
- Right attitude
- Clarity of values
- Clarity of direction
- Confidence in self
- Clear and competent articulation
- The ability to empathize
- Tolerance of ambiguity
- Feeling secure about oneself

Having these attributes can certainly get you started. You have the right set of qualities that a mentor should have at the outset. What you also need to look at are the details and the subtleties. Ask yourself these questions and see where you stand. Do you/are you

1. Actively interested in people? Yes/No
2. Believe ardently in and are passionate about people development? Yes/No
3. Enthusiastic about mentoring? Yes/No
4. Willing to invest time to help others? Yes/No
5. Prepared to learn even now from anybody? Yes/No
6. Always optimistic and positive? Yes/No
7. Always encouraging others? Yes/No

8. Have great reserves of patience?                          Yes/No
9. By nature approachable at any time,
   not intimidating?                                         Yes/No
10. Always honest and sincere in expressing
    your beliefs?                                            Yes/No
11. Open to new thoughts and ideas?                          Yes/No
12. Have the ability to be unbiased and
    objective?                                               Yes/No
13. Willing to accept your views being
    challenged?                                              Yes/No
14. Not expect that others should be like you?               Yes/No
15. Expert and good at your own job?                         Yes/No
16. Have achievements that make you a
    positive role model?                                     Yes/No
17. Have a good network of relationships
    and contacts?                                            Yes/No
18. A good active listener?                                  Yes/No
19. Not tell others only what they want
    to hear?                                                 Yes/No
20. Skillful at giving feedback?                             Yes/No
21. Non-judgmental and open-minded?                          Yes/No
22. Skillful and prudent in challenging
    assumptions?                                             Yes/No
23. Have the ability to draw out people and
    help them express ideas?                                 Yes/No
24. Willing to listen to the whole issue
    before making a comment?                                 Yes/No
25. Good at understanding the real issue
    through incisive questioning?                            Yes/No
26. Know when and how to suggest
    other options that people may not
    have considered?                                         Yes/No

27. Willing to consider mentees as equals?  Yes/No
28. Willing to help others realize their potential?  Yes/No
29. Willing to allow others to make their own decisions?  Yes/No
30. Open enough to allow others the freedom to make mistakes?  Yes/No
31. Inspire confidence to help others express their true feelings?  Yes/No
32. Take an active interest in people as individuals and value their opinions and views?  Yes/No
33. Keep in regular contact with those whom you work with or help?  Yes/No
34. Able to visualize the environment and scenario in which others live or work?  Yes/No
35. Not in a hurry to finish meetings with people whom you are helping?  Yes/No

If you have been able to answer most of these questions with 'yes,' then you are in a good position to move towards becoming a mentor. But do take the time to check on some of the other requirements listed below.

## Have you made a difference?

- At work, have you gone beyond planning the career of a junior colleague and helped her/him integrate personal and social life with work?
- Have you consciously worried about or helped work out life or community dilemmas of people within your sphere of influence?

- Do you feel the urge to help people live better lives?
- Do you invest time and energy in sorting out people's difficulties even when there is nothing in it for you or the issue has no connection with you?

If you have answered 'yes' to any of these questions, you are on a mission akin to mentoring. You might want to get into it seriously and work towards more gratifying successes.

## WHERE DO WE FIND MENTORS?

Real-life mentors are not easy to find. If there is a felt need for a mentor and you feel that one would make a significant difference in your life, where would you go looking for one?

Mentors do not normally announce themselves. They are likely to be unobtrusive and self-effacing by nature. It is easy to miss them in the crowd of life.

Mentors are self-assured people. They are also almost always successful people, but they are not aggressive or pushy about their success. They are often helpful people who take pride in the successes of others.

Some ask for nothing in return. Others may have a need to be acknowledged. But mentoring is not about payment or remuneration. There is no material benefit that a true mentor would expect.

## THE LONG HISTORY OF MENTORING

The word 'mentor' has come into English from the Greeks. Mentor was among the minor characters in the elegant mythology that the Greeks built around the ancient happenings in their numerous island republics. Though his role was not significant in the legends put together around the Trojan War, the word has lived on because of his remarkable work.

In his epic *Iliad*, Homer writes, among many others, of Odysseus, king of Ithaca. Odysseus, restless for adventure, leaves his family and kingdom behind to fight in the Trojan War. He leaves behind his young son, Telemachus, under the tutelage and care of his childhood friend Mentor.

Mentor brings up the young prince, teaching him the art of statecraft. He teaches Telemachus the guile to survive internecine intrigues, and develops in him the panache to enforce his will over a kingdom of unruly clansmen. Mentor's role is essentially that of a father figure. With the prolonged absence of Odysseus, however, the rest of the royal household crumbles around his son. Pretenders and usurpers attempt to win over Penelope, the queen, and take over the kingdom. Much more was added to the legend of Mentor after the little that Homer himself wrote. Mentor was said to be an incarnation of the goddess Athena.

Mentor did a pretty fine job with Telemachus. It is said that the goddess Athena herself had appeared in the form of Mentor to hold the crumbling edifice of Odysseus's household together. The slow but sure growth of Telemachus, under the wise guidance of Mentor, from a young and unsure lad to a fine youth emphasizes the importance of such a guide's role in the life of any person.

In Western myth, legend and history there are numerous examples of mentor–mentee relationships: Socrates and Plato; Plato and Aristotle; Haydn and Beethoven; Freud and Jung. The list can be extended to the modern day and into the corporate world: Freddie Laker and Richard Branson; Peter Dundee and Joan Collins; Warren Bennis and Howard Shultz. A visit to the website www.mentor.ca will show you an exhaustive list from the modern-day Western corporate world.

The idea and the relationship is by no means an import from the West into India. Relationships such as this have existed in Indian myths and legends as well. These are as old as, if not older than, Homer's *Iliad*.

The *parampara* (tradition) of *Guru* and *Shishya* (teacher and pupil) is as old as Indian civilization. The kings and chieftains of earlier days in fact followed the practice of having their heirs grow to maturity and wisdom under the tutelage of learned sages.

The scriptures of ancient India document several such relationships and practices. The revered scriptures and *Vedas* even codify the norms for such relationships and prescribe the basic requirements. The legends and history of ancient Indian civilization, passed down orally, are replete with examples of mentoring.

Arjuna's relationship with Krishna stands among the best examples of mentoring relationships. The crucial message of wisdom—putting things in perspective when thinking is incapacitated by intolerable dilemmas—is what makes all the difference. The message itself has been immortalized in the Bhagavad Gita, but it is not just the message that is important here. What is important is the clarity it provided Arjuna in resolving the impasse he found his thinking sinking into in that situation.

At that critical point in the war against the Kauravas, Arjuna had to struggle with the decision to fight, weighing his sacred duty as a warrior against the sanctity of filial relationships. Krishna's intervention, even at that late stage, offered the much-needed direction in this ethical and moral impasse which helped Arjuna so much in making his decision. This changed the entire course of the war, and also influenced the moral and ethical codes in latter-day Bharat.

Krishna had the interests of Arjuna at heart. Accomplished and matchless at everything as he himself was, he chose to champion Arjuna in the war. The self-effacing humility of Krishna is the stuff that great mentoring is made of. Going beyond the role of teacher, friend, well-wisher, guide (and whatever other roles we would like to ascribe to him), Krishna touched the very soul of Arjuna in his understanding and clarity of direction.

In reciprocation, the reverence, respect, affection and gratitude that Arjuna had for Krishna does make for an ideal mentee–mentor relationship. The victory and success that Arjuna achieved in battle and life are celebrated as his, but whenever Arjuna is spoken of, Krishna is too.

We should also note that while Krishna and Arjuna have an enormously large share of attention, the Mahabharata also talks of Parasurama and Karna, and Shakuni and Duryodhana in this context. These are also great mentor–mentee relationships. They are, however, less widely discussed and eulogized, perhaps because these personages ended up on the losing side. They are, nevertheless, good examples of the mentor raising the mentee above the level of mediocrity.

Indian myths and legends are replete with such mentoring relationships. Sages have been mentors to kings and, according to some beliefs, to gods as well. The sages unselfishly shared their wisdom with their 'mentees.'

In ancient Indian history too there are excellent examples of such great relationships. The singular achievement of the ascetic Brahmin Kautilya is an admirable example. Engineering the ascension of Chandragupta Maurya, a *Vaishya*, to the Nanda throne, during a time when the prerequisite for royalty was *Kshatriya*-hood, was in itself a deed of greatness. Kautilya was a great mentor to Chandragupta Maurya. The excellent exposition of the guiles of statecraft by Kautilya in his *Arthashastra* (a book of practical advice for kings) has made his alternate name 'Chanakya' a synonym for guile and cleverness in modern Indian popular parlance. Through the *Arthashastra*, Kautilya has been the guiding spirit behind many a successful ruler and statesman over the ages.

Bairam Khan's role in the growth and upbringing of the greatest of the Mughal emperors, Akbar, is significant. The initial tutelage and mentoring of young Akbar by Bairam Khan played a vital role in the way Akbar re-established the Mughal Empire in all its glory, and in the greatness he himself achieved in later years.

In modern India too there have been great examples of successful mentoring relationships. Bal Gangadhar Tilak was a great inspirational mentor to a significant number of later freedom fighters. Mohandas K. Gandhi in later years filled his place in guiding an entire generation of Indian leaders.

Much has been written about the close bond between Mahatma Gandhi and the young Jawaharlal Nehru. Jawaharlal's growth and commitment to the cause of India's freedom blossomed under the tutelage of Gandhi.

There is also the underplayed relationship that Vallabhbhai Patel had with Gandhi. Patel's respect and adoration of his mentor was so great that he made many a sacrifice and decision he may not otherwise have liked to make.

Through the years, there have been numerous mentor–mentee relationships in Indian history. One can trace the process back to before the legend of Mentor in Greek mythology. In India some people may argue against the use of the word 'mentor' with reference to such relationships. Perhaps Guru would be more satisfactory from a nationalist viewpoint. Call it what you will, what is important is to understand the role, relationship and process—and to accord it the respect and reverence it should command.

## UNDERSTANDING A MENTOR'S ROLE

During the course of several score workshops for mentors, designed and conducted over the past seven years, there have been several common terms that have often come up in the initial definition by participants of the role and character of a mentor. Here are some of the oft-repeated ones.

| | | |
|---|---|---|
| Friend | Philosopher | Guide |
| Guru | Teacher | Coach |
| Experienced person | Role model | Specialist |
| Counselor | Advisor | Consultant |
| Facilitator | Coordinator | Director |
| Master | Leader | Informal boss |
| Caretaker | Advocate | Protector |
| | Godfather | |
| Elder | Guardian | Surrogate parent |

All these terms have specific meanings, and the roles in some way or other do overlap with that of a mentor. But then, none of these fully describe the role of a mentor. There is more to a mentor than any of these roles by itself.

The oft-referred-to and popular definition of a mentor is 'friend–philosopher–guide.' The mentor is all these—

and definitely more. A friend is a trusted person. There is no friendship without 'trust.' *Trust* is the cornerstone of mentoring and the mentoring process. The quality of trust between mentor and mentee determines the strength of the mentoring relationship. The mentor must most certainly be a friend.

> The quality of TRUST determines the strength of the mentoring relationship.

A philosopher is one who can rise above the immediate and is able to visualize the larger implication of issues and events. She/he is one who can at the same time delve deep into the matter and have a broad view of the subject, the ability to conceptualize the issue and put things in proper perspective. The mentor has to do this all the time. This is the core part of the role.

> Conceptualizing the issue and putting things in the proper perspective—the mentor has to do this all the time.

The mentor is definitely a guide. The mentor may, like the guide, show the direction and the best way to get to the destination. But the mentor does not necessarily travel with the mentee on that journey. She/he may be a few paces behind, but the mentee must walk the distance herself/himself. Proper guidance at the appropriate time is the hallmark of a good mentor. Then again, the mentor is more than just a guide.

> Proper guidance at the appropriate time is the hallmark of a good mentor.

On the other hand, 'teacher' is an extremely restrictive label when describing a mentor. The mentor is definitely a teacher, but goes well beyond being just a teacher. The teacher has the agenda of ensuring learning in the chosen area of study and limits her/his role to just that. But the mentor goes beyond this in also helping configure the mentee's life to suit the overall goals that have been set.

Coaching is surely part of the role of the mentor, but that is just one part of the mentor's responsibility. A coach is often the person associated with the acquisition and honing of a particular skill. A coach is well-versed in the working of that particular aspect. The focus of the coach is on taking the person toward becoming the best in that particular skill or area. The relationship is also restricted to the duration of that particular activity and agenda. The mentor's canvas is much wider, encompassing most areas of the mentee's life.

The primary and most distinctive factor that makes a coach great rather than merely good is that in the course of developing the person under her/his care, the coach is not at any time threatened by the person's success or overcome by the fear of being overtaken in the application of that particular skill or specialization in the particular field. The mentor, like the coach, does not at any time feel threatened by the successes of the mentee. They are both secure in their own achievements and position.

> The mentor, like the coach, does not at any time feel threatened by the successes of the mentee.

Guru is a pretty accurate definition of a mentor: revered and respected above all others. Indian tradition and culture places a high premium on this relationship, equating it with the relationship with God. Paying respect to the Guru before starting any new enterprise or practice is the done thing in the Indian tradition.

The Indian belief regarding this role is more akin to the definition of a mentor. However, the current meaning attributed to the term Guru is restricted to the narrower implication of specialization in a chosen field. This restricts the applicability of the term to the mentor's role. The mentor's role is not restricted to any particular field or activity. Like the traditional Guru, the mentor touches large spans of a person's life. The mentor is thus a Guru in the traditional Indian sense of the word.

> The mentor is a *Guru* in the traditional Indian sense of the word.

Experienced person, role model, specialist—the mentor could be all these. This also implies that the mentor need not necessarily be any of these. Being an experienced person in the relevant line of work or area of interest is certainly of immense help; it is better still if one is a specialist; and finally, nothing can be more inspirational than being a role model. It is great for the mentor to be all these, but these roles do not cover the relationship that the mentor shares with the mentee. Thus these terms, used by themselves, fall short in defining the mentor's role.

Then there are many other roles that are often used to make comparisons with the role of a mentor: advisor, consultant, counselor, facilitator, coordinator, director. These are all roles that the mentor will at some time or the other have to play, during the course of the work she/he has taken on. Understanding when the mentor should play which role is the key capability and instinct of the mentor.

These are all roles that require the person to be an expert in her/his specific area and also have good human relations skills. They share the common thread of a thoughtful person studying an issue or problem in depth. Then come the differences between these roles.

> The mentor is an expert in her/his specific area and also a person with good human relations skills.

The *advisor* would offer one solution or option to be taken, which would in her/his considered opinion be the best. The recipient may take the advice or ignore it. The *consultant* on the other hand offers several options or solutions and may also suggest one of them as a preferred one for the recipient to consider. The term 'advisor' implies a closer relationship than 'consultant.'

The *counselor* does not offer any solutions herself/himself. The approach here is to help the 'client' articulate and clarify the issue or the problem. The counselor then helps the client seek and find her/his own solutions during the process of the interaction. The counselor is highly skilled in building trust, gaining insights and drawing the client out.

The *facilitator* is a helper in working towards a solution to contentious issues and problems that need to be negotiated between people. Facilitation is a skill of great importance in managing relationships and problem solving. The mentor needs this skill in great abundance. Also, being able to co-ordinate and negotiate solutions when they are not readily apparent makes the mentor a coordinator as well. As a director of all the interventions, and effectively of the relationship, the mentor needs to have the ability to keep a clear head and a grasp on the goings-on and the stage and position the process is in. But the mentor needs to be more than just a facilitator, coordinator or director; or even all of them put together.

Now we begin to cross the threshold into areas that the mentor must tread with extreme caution. The mentoring relationship is ideally one devoid of any power dynamics. There is always mutuality in all aspects of the relationship and the positions are clear and well accepted. The appearance of any form of power and authority structure tends to bring with it a subtle need to be cautious and less open in the relationship. This also tends to vitiate the relationship, with the focus often shifting to 'winning,' away from its mutual nature and developmental goals.

The term 'leader,' when used to define the mentor, may in a small way be representative in that there is an expectation that the mentor, being ahead of the mentee, is in many ways expected to take the lead. But the term also carries with it the baggage of implied authority and power, which makes its application to the mentor untenable.

The term 'master' aspect is way off the mark. The mentee does not have a relationship of servitude towards the mentor, and the obedience that the mentor commands is certainly not born out of the power and authority structure in the relationship. If there are any power and authority issues encroaching on the relationship between a mentor and a mentee, then the relationship is something other than a mentoring one.

> If there are any power and authority issues encroaching on the relationship between a mentor and a mentee, then the relationship is something other than a mentoring one.

The mentor is definitely not a caretaker, protector or advocate. These roles are by no stretch of imagination part of the mentor's responsibility. The mentoring process is envisaged as a developmental one and is unquestionably not an exploitative one. There may however be some of those who profess to be mentors while consciously or inadvertently slipping into taking on these roles. Make no mistakes about it—this is not mentoring. The mentees expecting or maneuvering to garner some advantage through such roles are seeking unfair exploitation of the mentoring process. This must be put down and stringently avoided.

> The mentor is definitely not a caretaker, protector, or advocate.

Such practices are detrimental to the entire mentoring process and the fair name of the mentor. Even in the Indian tradition and *parampara*, such practices have been frowned upon at and condemned as failings in a *Guru*. In the modern-day organization, the effects of such practices can be devastating for the organizational culture and environment. The organization will in a short period of time get split up into several patronage cliques, and the organizational system will head towards a slow death. Under the guise of mentoring, each caretaker, protector or advocate will reach out to foster her/his own ward and the organizational atmosphere will become geared towards a testing ground of the strengths of the various so-called 'mentors' rather than the merits and capability of the individual mentees. Not at all a good scenario!

## Case study 2.1    Targeting 'my' boy...

Ranjit Singh is after all my boy ... he has been with me for the past decade, and I have seen him grow ... I have actually brought him up. What would he have been otherwise? He has been my shadow for this past decade. I have taken him through the best of experiences ... exposed him to the most enriching experiences, and of course he has made use of them well. But it was all my doing ... everybody knows this....

Now, when they do this to him ... they must be targeting me. Surely there must be something in it. They don't have the guts to come after me, so they are going after the poor boy. *My* boy ... how dare they!

It must be those fellows working for Arun Lal ... he is himself a scoundrel. I wonder how he managed to get to the level of Deputy MD ahead of all of us. I should have fixed him last year before he got the elevation through his *chamchagiri* (sycophancy).

Ranjit Singh has been implicated in a case of showing undue favor in the decision he had taken to award the earthwork contract to his old acquaintance from his home district in western Uttar Pradesh. As the head of the department, he had the authority to take a decision in the matter, but there were set procedures, which, it was found on preliminary enquiry, had been overlooked. The order from headquarters to institute a formal enquiry had just come in. Ranjit Singh had called his 'mentor,' Ramesh Chander, the Regional Director (West) of the company based in Mumbai. This was a serious matter and he did not want it to get out of hand.

Ranjit had in fact bent some rules in awarding the contract, a major one, to his old friend. 'But then, this was the common practice in the company, everybody knows

CONTINUED ON THE NEXT PAGE

CASE STUDY 2.1—CONTINUED

it. Why am I being targeted?' He thought, 'Rameshji will be able to help. I have done so much for him when I have been with him over the past several years ... he is surely more powerful than all of those midgets sitting in HQ. I'm sure he will find a way.'

There are pitfalls for both mentor and mentee when the relationship moves away from mentoring and follows an unhealthy pattern.

The most common misconception is the interchange-ability perceived by many people in the roles of 'mentor' and 'godfather.' While the original meaning of the term godfather and the role ascribed to such a person in the Roman Catholic Christian faith is most honorable, the current status is something else altogether. In popular consciousness, the term today has a meaning given to it by the practices of the Mafia outlined in Mario Puzo's book, *The Godfather*. The term 'godfather' has today come to imply someone who bails you out of trouble, no matter how deep you are in it, and who watches out for you no matter what form of nefarious activity you are into. This is not good for a role that started out as being a sort of spiritual guardian, most respected and held very dear. This is definitely not a mentor's role.

The term 'godfather' today implies someone who bails you out of trouble, no matter how deep you are in it, and who watches out for you no matter what form of nefarious activity you are into. This is definitely not a mentor's role.

The mentor is ideally an elder, respected for the experience that she/he has garnered, revered as an elder in Indian culture and tradition. But being an elder is not an essential attribute of a mentor. The mentor may even be someone younger than you; someone in a different job setting (maybe lower than the mentee); or even someone in an unconnected area. Whether she/he has the other requisite attributes, capabilities and skills is what really counts.

All people have three crucial major aspects in their lives: the personal, the social, and the professional. In each of these, there is usually someone who takes us by the hand and leads us through the maze, showing us the paths. These are the three crucial roles in any person's life. In some cases they may be fused into one or two. In some cases, one or more of these may be missing. When any of these is missing, the absence is surely felt.

In one's personal life there are the parents. The parent takes care of growth and development in the personal aspects of life. This happens in the very early stages in everybody's life. The parent is concerned with the person growing up to have a good and safe personal life, and takes all the care needed to ensure that the best of health and happiness is bestowed upon the person in her/his personal life. Taking care of the health and well-being of the individual is often the role that falls within the purview of the role of the parent.

The social aspect of a person's development is taken care of by a guardian. The guardian looks into the development and progress of the individual in her/his interface and interaction with the society and the social environment. The guardian tries to ensure that the person has a well-adjusted personality, adequate social skills and a comfortable environment in which relationships and social associations are developed. The guardian is a role taken up to help the person socialize herself/himself into the social setting, with the right kind of values, attitudes and outlook to be a socially accepted and respected individual.

And then there is the professional aspect of the person's life. This has to do with the work environment and the career that the person has chosen to get into. Here comes the role of the mentor. The mentor helps the person develop and grow in her/his professional life, in terms of developing the personality, skills, qualities, outlook, and attitudes to be successful in professional life. The role that the mentor plays here has much to do with the kind of professional life the person has chosen or the kind of professional environment that exists. While the parent is concerned with the person's personal life and the guardian with her/his social life, the mentor concerns herself/himself with the professional aspects of the person's life.

The three roles may be distinct and separate from each other, or may, as in most cases, have substantial areas of overlap. The individuals playing these roles may be different, or there may be one or two people covering the three roles. However, it is to be understood that the roles are not unconnected with each other.

> While the parent is concerned with the person's personal life and the guardian with the social life, the mentor concerns herself/himself with the professional aspects of the person's life.

The parent role focuses on personal development, while using the social and the professional aspects to support development on the personal front. The guardian role focuses on the social development aspect, using the personal and professional aspects to shore this up. The mentor role has its focus on the professional development and growth of the person, while obtaining support from the personal and social aspects.

When the three roles are being played by different individuals in a person's life, it is most essential that they work in conjunction with one another and, as far as possible, interact closely. This is a healthy practice and goes a long way towards averting any form of conflict and misunderstanding between the most important people in a young person's life.

## A COMPARISON OF THE MENTOR WITH SOME OTHER ROLES

The roles of coach, counselor, and teacher/trainer are often compared with that of the mentor, especially in the organizational context. There are specific differences that set the mentor apart from the others, as described in the table below.

|  | Mentor | Coach | Counselor | Teacher/ Trainer |
|---|---|---|---|---|
| Client | Mentee | Organization/ Ward | Client | Organization/ Participant |
| Time-line | Long | Intermediate | Problem-oriented | Short |
| Focus | Growth | Performance enhancement | Problem solving | Learning and development |
| Emphasis | Relationship/ Development | Performance | Process | Delivery |
| Initiative | Bilateral | Coach | Client | Organization |

CONTINUED ON THE NEXT PAGE

TABLE—CONTINUED

|  | Mentor | Coach | Counselor | Teacher/ Trainer |
|---|---|---|---|---|
| Cost | None | May involve cost | May involve cost | Yes |
| Basis | Trust/ Inspiration | Capability | Trust | Capability/ Technique |
| WIIFM (What's In It For Me) | Altruism/Desire to share | Pride in self | Helping | Profession |
| Gain | Mutual | More by the client | Client | Client |
| Solution/ Approach/ Work | Mutual | More by the coach | More by the client | Trainer |
| Direction | Non-directional | Directional | Non-directional | Both |
| Power balance | Equal | One-sided (in favor of coach) | One-sided (in favor of client) | One-sided (in favor of trainer) |
| Initiation | Mutual | Either | Either | Organization |
| Gratification | Intangible | Intangible | Intangible or tangible | Tangible |
| Take-home | Values/Character/Personality development | Skill | Problem solving | Skill/ Knowledge |

# DEFINITIONS OF MODERN-DAY MENTORING IN ORGANIZATIONS

There is a strong and influential difference in the way American corporate culture views mentors and the Europeans view them. Americans tend to lean strongly towards looking at the mentor as a sponsor and guarantor of the mentee. They appear to view them as people who work to further and in a sense carry the career of the chosen mentee. In the mentoring practices in the accepted American corporate culture, there is also an all-or-nothing attached to the way the mentor puts the mentee forward.

The American system is often referred to as the 'Sponsoring School of Mentoring.' In the late 1960s, Ralph M. Stodgill referred to the mentor as 'an ambitious authority figure' (quoted in Clutterbuck 2001). Dr. Audrey Collins in 1979 gave the definition as 'influential people who significantly help you reach your life goals.' Authority appears to be a strong factor in the relationship and the connection to the organizational setting.

The European approach tends to lean more towards the developmental side of the process. They appear to see the purpose of mentoring as being 'to help and support people to manage their own learning in order to maximize their potential, develop their skills, improve their performance, and become the person they want to be,' as defined by Eric Parsloe. Jenny Sweeney contributes this definition on her website:

> Mentoring is a partnership between two people built on trust. It is a process in which the mentor offers ongoing support and developmental opportunities to the mentee. Addressing issues and blockages identified by the mentee, the mentor offers guidance, counseling and support in the form of pragmatic and objective assistance. Both share a common purpose of developing a strong two-way learning relationship.

There are several definitions of mentoring, most complimenting one another, offering different perspectives on who or what a mentor is. Although they are applied largely to the organizational context, by no means do restrict themselves to operating within the confines of organizations.

These definitions are quoted from the free compilation by Andrew Gibbons on his website, www.andrewgibbons. co.uk:

Mentoring is a supportive learning relationship between a caring individual who shares knowledge, experience and wisdom with another individual who is ready and willing to benefit from this exchange, to enrich their professional journey (Suzanne Faure).

Mentoring is a long term relationship that meets a development need, helps develop full potential, and benefit all partners, mentor, mentee and the organization (Suzanne Faure).

Mentoring is a protected relationship in which learning and experimentation can occur, potential skills can be developed, and in which results can be measured in terms of competencies gained (Audrey Collins).

The purpose of mentoring is to help the mentee to change something—to improve their performance, to develop their leadership qualities, to develop their partnership skills, to realise their vision, or whatever. The movement from where they are (here) to where they want to be (there) (Mike Turner).

Mentoring does not happen by accident, nor do its benefits come quickly. It is relationally based, but it is more than a friendship.... Mentoring is not two people spending time together sharing (Thomas Addington and Stephan Graves).

| Case study 2.2 | Rachna Varma's party |
| --- | --- |

Rachna Varma couldn't remember a happier day. She had just returned from partying late into the night with her office colleagues and friends. This was an occasion that

CONTINUED ON THE NEXT PAGE

CASE STUDY 2.2—CONTINUED

couldn't have gone any other way. She had let her hair down and really went out to enjoy herself ... everybody else did too. And they showed it effusively. It was her party, and a big one at that.

She sank back into the comfort of the couch and stretched as she ran over the events of the day through her mind. There was just one thing that ran over and over again, filling her with warmth and making her smile to herself. With eyes closed she threw her head back and almost screamed her joy out....

This was something she had always looked forward to. And she was finally here. It was her dream playing itself out. Long ago, she had set herself the goal of heading a recognized and major organization. To be looked up to and have the power to make a difference. This was the first day of that phase. She had called for a celebration on her being officially appointed the head of the India operations of the international HR consulting house.

Rachna had small dreams as a young postgraduate in social work. She had hoped for a good comfortable job with a company that had a large enough workforce that could give her contribution a meaning. She had hoped to make a difference to people whom she worked with. A secure job, and then to build a life around it. It meant little to her that she had topped the university.

That was quite long ago and Rachna did not forget the moments that had changed so much of all that. That was her coming to work with Mr. Ashok Hegde, then the DGM (HR) in the pharmaceutical MNC outside Mumbai.

Ashok Hegde was in the beginning a really hard person to work with. He had been a tough head of department at the plant. He had always kept everybody on their toes, pushing them to do better and was almost never satisfied

CONTINUED ON THE NEXT PAGE

CASE STUDY 2.2—CONTINUED

with anything of their working. Quite a few had left the organization because of that. But Rachna remembers Hegde saying that those who survive him will be the best in what they do, and will thank him for being tough with them. That, Rachna had realized much later, was the tough front he presents. It is the other side that makes all the difference.

Hegde was at core a people development person. He had pushed Rachna, sometimes to the point of her detesting him, to look at her strengths and not settle for anything less. He has goaded Rachna to get out of the welfare function she had been so comfortable in and move into other functions in the HR department.

There were times when she was terrified of the work she was asked to take up. She remembers well the domestic enquiry she had to conduct on the pilferage charges against a tough workman. She had cried and even spent the night without sleep over this. She had almost given in to her fears and resigned. But Hegde would not let her. He had hand-held and walked her through the task. That was one hard learning experience she would not forget.

This had, in retrospect, made all the difference. Rachna had to shake awake the dormant abilities she had of learning afresh in new areas she found herself posted in. Hegde had supported her professionally in those four hard years. She had almost stumbled through learning HR as a professional rather than being a fringe player.

It was in this that she came on to her own. Ashok Hegde had taught her to dream big and not settle for anything less than what she was capable of achieving. He had shown her what she was capable of.

Hegde had gone on to head the HR function in the MNC as director. Rachna had changed two organizations

CONTINUED ON THE NEXT PAGE

CASE STUDY 2.2—CONTINUED

since then—each time a substantial growth in status and function—until she settled in with the HR consulting organization, initially in charge of their recruitment division, and now heading the entire operation. All the time she had been in touch with Hegde and he had encouraged her to go for things she often felt were beyond her.

Now, after the celebration, what made her feel on top of the world was that she had seen Ashok Hegde do something she never thought he would do for anything or anyone ... dance at her party!

## WHAT IT TAKES TO BE A MENTOR

Andrew Gibbons has made quite an exhaustive collection of thoughts of scholars and practitioners on what it takes to be a mentor.

[A mentor is] an accomplished and experienced performer who takes a special, personal interest in helping to guide and develop a junior or more inexperienced person (Stephan Gibb).

A mentor facilitates personal and professional growth in an individual by sharing the knowledge and the insights that have been learned through the years. The desire to share these 'life experiences' is the characteristic of a successful mentor (Arizona National Guard).

A mentor is someone who patiently assists with someone's growth and development in a given area. This assistance can come in the form of guidance, teaching, imparting of wisdom and experience (Chicago Computer Society).

A Mentor is a more experienced individual willing to share knowledge with someone less experienced in a relationship of mutual trust (David Clutterbuck).

A great mentor has a great knack of making us think that we are better than we think we are. They force us to have a good opinion of ourselves, let us know they believe in us. They make us get more out of ourselves, and once we learn how good we really are, we never settle for anything less than our very best (The Prometheus Foundation).

These and many more definitions of mentoring can be found at www.andrewgibbons.co.uk.

| Case study 2.3 | The unkindest cut of all |
| --- | --- |

A long time ago, in the dense jungles of ancient India lived the young son of a tribal chieftain. His name was Ekalavya. This young boy always dreamed of becoming a great archer. One day, he made up his mind to make his dream come true. He set off, with his father's blessings, to one of the great cities of the time, Hastinapura, to meet Acharya Drona, who was the acknowledged expert in archery and the martial arts.

Acharya Drona was at that time in the employ of the mighty king of Hastinapura, teaching the young princes the fine art of archery. Ekalavya called on Acharya Drona at the palace where the Acharya stayed. Ekalavya implored Acharya Drona to accept him as a disciple. Acharya Drona was quite impressed by the desire and the keenness of the youth to learn and master the art.

Acharya Drona saw some of the skills Ekalavya had and was quite impressed. He enquired about the background of Ekalavya. On learning that Ekalavya was the son of a tribal chieftain and a *sudra* (the lowest social community), Acharya Drona was enraged that Ekalavya would dare to approach him to be his *Guru*. He had Ekalavya ejected from the palace right away.

CONTINUED ON THE NEXT PAGE

CASE STUDY 2.3—CONTINUED

Ekalavya was hurt deeply by the behavior of Acharya Drona. He was upset to see the other students of Acharya Drona look at him scornfully and mock his desire to learn. Acharya Drona's angry words caused him great pain, but this did not dishearten Ekalavya. He was determined to master the art and become a great archer himself. He was convinced that Acharya Drona was a *Guru* to him and he could learn archery.

Ekalavya returned to the forest and settled down in a small clearing. Here he made a clay mage of Acharya Drona and treated it as his *Guru*. He prayed to it, offered it flowers and sought its blessings before setting forth to practice archery. He practiced day and night with the single-minded resolve to be the best.

One day the princes from Hastinapura were out hunting with their teacher, Acharya Drona, in the nearby forest. One of their hunting dogs wandered towards the clearing where Ekalavya was practicing. The dog started to bark loudly on seeing Ekalavya.

Ekalavya was disturbed by the dog barking. Angered with the disturbance, but not wanting to hurt the animal, Ekalavya shot arrows in the direction of the sound. The arrows struck the mouth of the dog in such a way that it could not bark, but did not hurt it. The dog slunk back to the camp of the princes.

Acharya Drona and the princes were amazed at the skill of the archer who could silence the dog without hurting it, locating it merely by its barking. They carefully removed the arrows and the dog led them to the clearing where Ekalavya was practicing his art.

The princes were envious of Ekalavya's skill. Acharya Drona, not remembering Ekalavya from their past meeting, asked him who his *Guru* was. Ekalavya paid his respects

CONTINUED ON THE NEXT PAGE

CASE STUDY 2.3—CONTINUED

to Acharya Drona, saying that the great Acharya was himself his *Guru*. Acharya Drona asked Ekalavya to prove himself in competition with the princes whom Acharya Drona had him-self personally taught.

Ekalavya accepted and was quick in defeating each one of the princes, including Arjuna, the expert archer. This upset Acharya Drona, and he was angry that even his favorite disciple Arjuna was defeated.

Blinded by rage, Acharya Drona said that since Ekalavya had accepted Drona as his Guru, Ekalavya must give him *guru-dakshina* (a disciple's tribute to the *Guru* for teaching). Ekalavya gladly agreed to give Acharya Drona anything he asked for. Out of spite, Acharya Drona asked for Ekalavya's right thumb. Without hesitation, Ekalavya drew his sword, cut off the thumb from his right hand and offered it to his *Guru*.

Acharya Drona returned to Hastinapura, content in the thought that he had incapacitated the only competition to Arjuna. Little did he feel for Ekalavya, the most faithful disciple of all time.

# 3

# THE MENTORING PROCESS

HAVING got a fix on who a mentor could be and what various people think the mentor is, let us get to what a mentor does, especially in an organizational context. Let us take a walk-through to understand what the process entails, and what it is all about.

## IN THE BEGINNING—THE CONTACT

The mentoring process often actually begins with a simple contact. This is where a mentor and the prospective mentee meet, perhaps for the first time. This meeting may be formal or casual. Long years later, in retrospect, the beginning of the relationship can be traced back to this meeting.

There is nothing special about this contact and it may slip away from memory. Perhaps years later in calm times, one may reflect and retrace the seed of a successful relationship to this contact. The unfortunate part is that because one meets so many people in the course of life, this meeting may fade into the by-lanes of memory soon after it happens and may not actually register as important.

The contact may turn out to be a non-event with nothing happening worthy of record. It may merely contribute to the awareness of one another. There may not be any calculation or intent that it may turn out to be anything of significance.

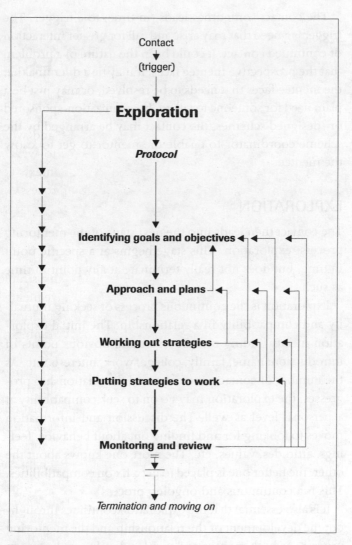

**Figure 3.1**
The mentoring process

The contact sometimes leads, in time, to a trigger. The trigger is a need that may arise and call for greater interaction or continued contact. It could be in the nature of a problem that the prospective mentee faces. It may be a dilemma that the mentee faces that needs to be resolved, or may just be a plain need for someone to talk to. In organization-sponsored or -designed schemes, the contact may be arranged by the scheme coordinator to enable the mentor to get to know the mentee.

## EXPLORATION

The contact then leads into the next stage of the mentoring process: exploration. This stage begins at a specific point in time, but does not really terminate at any point in time as such.

Exploration is the continuous process of seeking mutuality and compatibility in a relationship. The initial exploration means finding out the overt and obvious points of introduction: name, family, college, work, interests, etc. As the number of contacts increases and the relationship progresses, the exploration may go on to seek compatibility at a personal level as well. The discussion and information moves to looking for and finding out about behavior, feelings, attitudes, values, etc. The more one knows about the other, the better one is placed to get a fix on compatibilities. This is a continuous and ongoing process.

It is also essential that the exploration continues throughout the development of the relationship and the mentoring process. As both mentor and mentee develop and grow in experience and understanding, there are new aspects to each person that emerge. There is always the need to understand these new and emerging aspects as well. The ability to share and help share is one of the cornerstones of successful relationships. It also helps both the people to grow together and evolve in similar directions rather than drift apart.

## THE PROTOCOL

One essential step that must come appropriately early is the arrival at a mutually accepted 'protocol' in the relationship. The 'protocol' is no more than a code of conduct with each other: a clarification of expectations and boundaries within which the relationship will function, the parameters of the relationship and the expectations from it.

The protocol is something that cannot be taken to be 'understood.' It is important to articulate it to ensure that it is understood as such and not subject to misinterpretation, extending the intended meaning of any of the aspects of the relationship. It is good to tell each other from time to time what the expected behaviors and norms are and what is not acceptable.

Very often the first issue that needs to be worked out is the very meaning of being a mentor or a mentee. How does each perceive the role? How does each plan to align the meanings and how does each intend to reconcile the differences in the way they perceive mentoring itself?

Then there is the issue of each person's expectations from the mentoring process and how far each is willing or wants to go in that process. The mentor may have one set of limits that she/he intends to put into place, while the mentee may have other ideas. This would need to be especially carefully applied to the kind of assistance that can be expected to accrue from the relationship. The mentor is not a 'godfather,' and being a 'protector' is not the expected role. This must be adequately clear to both mentor and mentee. The clarity must emerge that the mentor will do this much, and that the mentee should not expect to be taken care of beyond that. This understanding must be mutual and articulated as a protocol to safeguard the relationship and the progress of mentoring.

The protocol is not a one-time creation set in stone. It is definitely mutually negotiated and accepted, but also subject to modifications and dynamic evolution as the relationship progresses. With the continued exploration and the affirmation of mutual trust between mentor and mentee, the protocol may need to undergo amendment, modification and revision. All this is to be shared and mutually accepted. The existence of the protocol gives the mentoring relationship a structure and a sense of formality. And then again, the fact that the protocol is fluid and dynamic helps the relationship remain open and flexible, and allows it to develop.

The protocol also helps in constructing and clarifying the context of the relationship and the responsibilities of both sides, making sure that the relationship stays within the proper bounds and does not veer away from the original purpose at any time. In a sense, it puts to rest the niggling fear either party may have in the initial phases of the relationship that they may deliberately or inadvertently be taken advantage of in the process of being open. The continuation of the mutual exploration of the process, along with the comfort of the protocol, contributes to strengthening the relationship.

## Case study 3.1 | Two bottles of DM water

The day had not been too busy. It had gone off pretty well, with not too many decisions to be taken. And those that had to be taken had worked out quite well and you could well be appreciated for them. You smile at the thought.

You also managed to get quite a few routine matters out of the way, even the two thorny cases that had been on your desk for about a week.

You are unwinding, preparing to shut down and leave for home. Earlier today than on other days—in fact, the earliest you can recall for the past two years you have been DGM (Operations) at the plant.

The phone rings, and you wonder who it could be. You were not expecting any call at this time. You reach forward and pick up the phone.

'Advani sir?' the voice enquires.

'Yes,' you reply.

'Senior Inspector Jaya Prakash speaking, sir, from the main gate,' the voice announces, 'we have stopped Ravi Kumar here, sir. He told us your name, sir. We have seized two bottles of DM water from his scooter, sir,' and the voice pauses.

'One minute,' you tell him. You look up to see that your secretary has just entered your room.

'Two bottles of DM water?' you find yourself asking, what the devil would Ravi be doing taking DM water out of the plant?

Ravi Kumar has been your mentee for just over three months now. He is a Graduate Engineer in the Maintenance Department. Bright and energetic, you have begun to like him and have appreciated his enthusiasm to learn.

But DM water... demineralized water is probably the most innocuous thing in a continuous process plant. At

CONTINUED ON THE NEXT PAGE

CASE STUDY 3.1—CONTINUED

best, it could be used in a car battery, and would anyway be easily available at any petrol pump for just about Rs. 20.

But taking any material out of the plant without written authorization from the 'competent authority' is not permitted, and is tantamount to an offence. Everyone knows that.

Your forehead knits up in a frown, as you wonder …
What is your next move? What will you do?

CONTINUED AT THE END OF THIS CHAPTER

The heart of the mentoring process lies in the next few stages, which relate to the purpose behind our going into this at all. All the mentor's wisdom and experience come into focus here, and the ability of the mentee to work with clarity and a sense of purpose are crucial at this point.

When the mentor (and ideally the mentee too) feels that their mutual trust is adequately strong and their relationship is on an even keel, they may venture into working on the first step in the core purpose of mentoring: identifying the mentee's ambitions, goals, and objectives.

There is one caution that must be flagged here. The exploration and seeking of mutual comfort and trust is definitely essential to the success of the process and the relationship, but this should not in itself become the focus and meander along for too long. What is a reasonable time and course is difficult to prescribe as a one-size-fits-all kind of decree. It is really the mentor's call when she/he feels the time is good to take the next step.

This is almost always not a one-sitting, one-step activity. It may take a few or several contacts and sessions to be adequately sure that both have sufficient clarity on the matter to make the move forward. A series of dialogs on what the mentee intends to do with herself/himself are required. What does she/he want to achieve in life? Where does she/he want to find herself/himself after a period of time? How realistic are these visions of herself/himself? Do the various plans tie in together? Are any of the plans working at cross-purposes ? How prepared is the mentee to work towards what she/he plans for herself/himself? These questions, and those that may follow consequently, once tackled help attain a certain level of clarity.

The mentor may use any approach or technique to get the mentee to identify, clarify, and then to refine her/his goals. In the larger dimension, this means identifying what the mentee's ambitions are in her/his profession and life, and how they have helped frame the goals. Through careful questioning and searching, the mentor must help the mentee sort through the maze of desires that may cloud her/his vision, and help her/him zero in on the crucial and actionable ambitions and goals. This stage is the key, in that it is from here that the specifics of the strategy and plans for the mentee will emerge.

| Case study 3.2 | Just one call away ... |
| --- | --- |

He had already punched out the number three times. Each time, he had canceled it without dialing. The fourth time he did dial, but cut the call before it rang. He sat there hoping that it hadn't gone across as a missed call ... it would definitely not make too good an impression. But what could he do? Should he call?

Gopinathan Srinivasan's predicament was something he did not know how to handle. Pretty unusually for

CONTINUED ON THE NEXT PAGE

CASE STUDY 3.2—CONTINUED

Srini, he was stumped. Strange, he thought, even Mr. Bharadwaj had called him Srini from the very first meeting. Bharadwaj Sir had been so approachable. Then why was he hesitating?

Srini had felt that he did not need Bharadwaj. He had got by quite well so far, or so he thought. But there was a part of him that kept telling him that he wasn't doing quite as well as he thought. He wasn't sure which voice to listen to.

One voice screamed at him loudly from inside, goading him into believing that he himself was the best judge of what was good for himself. He could make decisions for himself ... after all, he had put in two good years studying to become an ace decision-maker. He had done phenomenally well in the past years in his career too, or so he felt. So he should be able to apply the technique to himself. So what if the choice was between what was good for his career and what was good for the organizations he worked with? His evaluation and approach to the decision was after all impeccable.

Srini was brilliant. That was never in doubt. He had aced the examinations all through school, setting an enviable record, a record that would perhaps not be approached for long years to come. He had almost waltzed into the IIT top ranks in the all-India list. The years at IIT were a song too ... he topped his batch all through. After briefly toying with the idea of an MS at an American university, he had decided to move out of engineering, and hit upon taking a management degree at the postgraduate level.

So IIM was the logical choice. The CAT exam was nothing more than a necessary formality for him. The question was whether he would top it or someone else

CONTINUED ON THE NEXT PAGE

would beat him to it. Well … someone did. Actually two of them did, but that didn't matter too much eventually, as he had all the IIMs to choose from. Srini chose to go to Ahmedabad and there he had the satisfaction of beating the two who had got ahead of him in the CAT.

Four and a half years had passed since then. Srini had worked in three organizations—all top-rung multinationals— in different locations, including two foreign postings. In each organization, he had made his mark within a few months. The next few months saw offers flooding his desk as headhunters sought him out and vied with each other to snare him. He was back in India in his present job mainly because his widowed mother was in bad health and had insisted that she would only stay with him 'during her last days.' He had given in to her demand, although he felt that his sister and younger brother should have done something.

Srini was feeling the restlessness again. He had been in this organization for the past nine months. There was nothing new left for him to figure out here. He had cut everything down to bare-minimum routines in a matter of months, and then it was just a question of pulling the right strings to get the show going. He had done this so many times in the past. It no longer tested him and he could feel the slack.

Ananth Bharadwaj had come into his life during his final term at the IIM. Bharadwaj, with long years in the industry, had chosen to step off the bus and take the slower track in consulting and teaching. Choosing not to take a job, he had come as a visiting faculty to the IIM during Srini's final term. He was quite impressed with Srini, as Srini was with him. Bharadwaj was somebody who could break

CONTINUED ON THE NEXT PAGE

CASE STUDY 3.2—CONTINUED

through the cynical façade and get in touch with Srini's restless brilliance.

One hour of personal time with Bharadwaj in his office room, and Srini couldn't get Bharadwaj out of his mind. They hadn't talked about anything specific, just the aspects of the elective course that Bharadwaj was offering ... something about how the top students from the institute should make choices relating to themselves ... something about Srini's approach to his work and career ... nothing that Srini could specifically remember. But Bharadwaj had touched Srini as nobody else had.

Something made Srini speak to Bharadwaj periodically, every few months or so. That had continued over the period that Srini was outside India too. Srini sometimes called it his quarterly 'fix.' He somehow felt energized and had a greater clarity after speaking with Bharadwaj. But Srini sometimes also called this a weakness. Why should he have to speak with Bharadwaj to get this 'high'? He was surely capable of figuring out things himself?

And then there was this 'other' voice inside Srini too. This was a quieter one, more calm and sedate. This was the more rational one. This asked Srini to look at his career—he had led a peripatetic life so far. Tumbling from one place to another and one job to another, just because it was there for the taking and he had outgrown the previous one too fast. Where was this leading him? Bharadwaj would help him as he had done in the past.

Srini remembered that Bharadwaj always had this calm way of cutting through the rubble and getting to the heart of the matter. He had helped Srini clear his head so many times and enabled him to look at the path ahead. Srini also recalled that it was Bharadwaj who had suggested

CONTINUED ON THE NEXT PAGE

CASE STUDY 3.2—CONTINUED

that there was strength to be sought in the width of experience gathered in the many organizations and locations
that Srini had worked in.

Now that Srini was feeling the itch again, could he call
Bharadwaj? Should he do it? Can and will Bharadwaj help
this time too? What's in it for him? Shouldn't Srini be able
to work things out for himself by now? If not now, then
when? And, after all, what has Bharadwaj got that Srini
hasn't?

Srini sat with the phone in his hand. Bharadwaj's number
was already keyed in … Srini took one long hard look at
the phone and his finger moved towards the call button.

Here again, the mentor has to take a call on whether the
mentee is sufficiently clear about where she/he is headed
and is now in a better position to work out the details of
the strategy for the long-term and the immediate. The
mentor also has to figure out which of the ambitions and
goals are actionable now and which have to be mothballed
for later. This is where the sagacity and maturity of the
mentor help the mentee. The width of perception and the
long years of grappling with issues make the difference.

One thing that must be taken into account here is oft-
encountered temptation to let the goals and the identification of the direction remain loose, and to work on things
as they come up. There may be some benefits in this approach, very limited as they may be. But in the longer-
term interest of the relationship and the mentoring process,
it is better by far to have clarity and to be specific about the
life and professional goals. Working loosely and in an un-
structured relationship gives each greater freedom and re-
duces the chances of excessive dependence, but the process

generally tends to dilute itself down to something other than mentoring—advisor perhaps, or counselor—and becomes less focused on development.

There is also the vital role of the mentor in figuring out whether the goals—or, for that matter, the ambitions—of the mentee are justifiable and adequate. There may well be times when the mentee is quite capable of considerably-stretch more than what she/he visualizes herself/himself as being capable of. On the other hand, the mentee may sometimes well be overreaching herself/himself. This is where the mentor works to moderate and temper the ambitions and goals of the mentee, or pushes the mentee to aim higher.

This activity also involves taking an inventory of the capabilities and competencies of the mentee. In working out the strategies for achieving the set goals, a part would also be on how new capabilities, skills and competencies can be developed, and how existing ones can be strengthened. Working with competencies and capabilities is an important aspect of the process, and the mentor is better placed to help the mentee with such an inventory.

## WORKING OUT STRATEGIES

The next stage in the mentoring process is helping the mentee arrive at strategies to act on achieving her/his ambitions and goals, both professional and in life. First comes the process of helping the mentee get a fix on the overall plan and approach. This is essentially to tie in with the overall direction that the mentee should take in her/his career and profession.

This will help in identifying milestones to work towards in set periods of time. It is often a good idea to have these signposts in the career clearly identified, as they could well work as indicators on whether the progress is going well, or whether corrective revisions need to be put in place. Further, these signposts are the markers for working out the short- and intermediate-term plans for the mentee.

Where the mentor needs to come in is to help the mentee access activities and resources that will feed into development in the identified areas. The mentor would be in a better position to identify and help in deciding what kind of assignments, projects, roles, and postings the mentee should pitch for in order to grow in particular areas. The mentor can help the mentee build an adequate and convincing case for her/his being given those assignments. The mentor can also help identify what areas of the particular work the mentee should concentrate on to get the maximum return out of the work put in.

The mentor can also help the mentee network to access information and human resources that would help in this direction. The mentor would definitely be better placed to use her/his expertise to guide the mentee here.

The mentor's role may not be restricted to helping in working out the short-term and long-term strategies alone. Another crucial aspect that comes to the fore here is the way the mentor is able to keep the mentee on course while also keeping the larger picture in view.

## MID-COURSE REVIEW

Periodically, the mentor and the mentee need to take stock of how the effort, the work and the approach to set goals are progressing. Reviewing and taking stock is an important aspect of ensuring that the process stays on course.

What the periodicity of this process should be can be a mutual call, or can be determined by what the mentor may feel to be necessary. The review may be set to a specified schedule and period or be left ad hoc, depending on the nature of each plan and step that is afoot.

The review may lead to mid-course correction in plan and strategy, or may reaffirm what is already going on. In some cases, it may also help reassess goals and rework them as necessary. There may also be instances where certain goals and targets may be abandoned altogether. The review may also throw up a need for renewal and reworking of the whole process and working down the loop once again.

## TERMINATION AND MOVING ON

Possessiveness and ownership are not an issue in the scheme of things in mentoring. A mentee and a mentor do not 'belong' to each other. They are bound by the gossamer thread of admiration and respect, as well as well-being and pride in being associated with each other. The dull ache of separation comes in the field of love and has no place in mentoring.

There may come a time in the later part of mentoring association when there would be a mutual feeling that the mentee needs to branch out further and there isn't much more that the mentor can offer. This is a stage that comes up when the mentee has grown sufficiently, or has branched into other areas of interest and pursuit that are beyond the areas in which the mentor can offer any reasonable guidance. It could also be the case that the mentor has grown in a different direction.

It is here that the issue of termination comes in. There need not be a formal termination as such, as the relationship that has been built may be strong and will therefore endure. However, the context of mentoring may effectually be at an end. In any case, the decision should, like all else in mentoring, be mutual. The feeling of mutual respect and platonic affection, of professional association and goodwill, will and should no doubt continue. But the players in the process may have outgrown each other. This is the autumn of the mentoring process ....

| Case study 3.1 | Two bottles of DM water (continued) |
| --- | --- |

What would you do? What is your next move?

Would you tell Senior Inspector Jaya Prakash that it is only DM water and to let Ravi Kumar off? Would you go to the gate yourself? Would you ask to speak to Ravi Kumar? Would you call up your counterpart in the Maintenance Department (Ravi's boss) and ask him to intervene? Would you ask your secretary to handle the issue? Would you ask Senior Inspector Jaya Prakash to go by set procedures? What other options will you take?

Well ... you have a certain status in the organization and the Senior Inspector will do your bidding. You have a network in the organization and your counterpart will definitely do whatever you ask. And you can take the stand that it is after all only a question of two bottles of DM water. You can take any of these positions....

What you need to remember is that you are a mentor, not Ravi Kumar's boss. There is a set procedure in the organization to deal with any misdemeanor, of any magnitude. And the normal procedure under such circumstances would have been to intimate the reporting officer

CONTINUED ON THE NEXT PAGE

CASE STUDY 3.1—CONTINUED

of the individual concerned: the Head of the Maintenance Department. It is the line manager's call on what action is to be taken. As a mentor, you actually have no role till after the normal administrative process is complete.

The problem here is that the protocol between the mentor and the mentee has not been clearly enunciated, and it is not therefore not clearly understood that the mentor is not a protector and will not leverage his position to bail out the mentee in instances of transgression. In the absence of this clarity, and taking the safer and more convenient option, Ravi Kumar would have used your name in the hope of being protected. If you do protect him, there would be no difference between you as a mentor and a benign (mafia) godfather.

This is why a clear understanding of the role and protocol is important between the mentor and the mentee.

# 4

# THE MENTOR'S MIND

AM I really good at this? Is this for me at all? After all, why am I getting into this? What do I expect to establish? What am I looking to get out of it? What is the gratification I am seeking? All these questions and more…. What do I expect out of the mentee and/or the system? What is the nature of the outcome I am expecting from the mentee, the system and the process?

## GETTING IN TOUCH WITH VALUES

Values are positions or stands we take with regards to particular issues or aspects of life. These are fundamental to our outlook towards life in all its features, and govern the way we lead them. We espouse values that modulate the attitudes we have and eventually how we behave in a given situation or circumstance. Values are effectively the foundation of our lives, and how we build and lead our lives depends on the values we hold dear.

All values are positive. They configure the world around us and help us view it in a particular way in keeping with the way we have configured it. Our values, being positive, give us a positive orientation and approach to the world around us. This gives us an optimistic and sunny outlook on the various dimensions that life presents itself in.

There are numerous values in life, most of which we are not even aware of. They lie within us, only to become active when they are needed to guide our actions in particular situations or circumstances. When we encounter certain situations, the value (or values) relevant to guiding the decisions we need to make manifests itself and we could become aware of them. Otherwise they lay comfortably ensconced within us, leaving us oblivious to their existence.

However, values themselves are quite delicate and need to be nurtured and cared for at all times. The more often the values are supported when called into question, the more nourishment they get. But then, being delicate by themselves, they tend to erode easily as well. This happens when we work against them, in however small a way. And each slippage of this kind against any value makes the next slippage that much easier. Each erosion saps the strength of the value until it is no longer strong enough to stand up to the onslaught, and it ceases to be a value that we espouse.

Erosion of values and the consequent weakness of the values that govern our lives leads us into behaviors and practices that are negative and contrary to accepted norms and expectations. So it is not that negative values produce negative actions, but that weak and eroded values are unable to guide actions in the right direction. Espousing the right set of values, nurturing and tending them to keep them sturdy in the face of adversity, creates people of extraordinary fortitude.

The negative practices and behaviors—corruption, delinquency, sycophancy, and the like—are the result of values not being strong enough to resist the temptation to fall prey to these practices. It is after all a matter of choice: the choice of working to stick to the values and keeping them strong, or giving into temptation and lapses, leading to further erosion of values.

No justification is ever adequate to cover the compromise of values. It is a matter of making the right choice of staying with our values, facing adversity or hardship if necessary, or letting go of values. Attempting to cover the bad choice comes in the form of justifications like: 'Everybody does it'; 'To get ahead in life'; 'Society is responsible'; 'No other choice'; 'Not my fault'; and the list can go on....

The mentor comes in here. She/he is the bulwark preventing the mentee tumbling into compromises that might jeopardize the positive view she/he can hold of the profession, organization, world and eventually of life itself. Getting the mentee to imbibe and hold on to values that lead her/his life forward is the prime responsibility of the mentor.

For this to take an actionable form, the mentor has to get in touch with the values shaping her/his thoughts and outlook. Even with regard to settings not yet encountered, it augurs well for the mentor to establish and understand the values that direct her/him. The mentor has the responsibility of being prepared for most situations that may be encountered.

The mentor should ideally have clarity about the values she/he as an individual holds dear, and also the structure or system of values that the organization and the social system around espouse. Personal values are ones that she/he leads her/his life by, and at times they may be in conflict with those advocated by the organization or society. In this, we must properly understand the balance that has been achieved for these values to peacefully co-exist. All too often, the mentor finds herself/himself in a position where these issues need to be spoken about and clarified to the mentee in such a way as to make the mentee understand it too.

One more issue about values is that one also has to be prepared to handle conflicts in values between people. The situation becomes more complex where the conflict in values intrudes into relationships as well. It is here that the mentor's clarity of thought and capability to restore the balance without heading into dilution of values becomes vital.

It is a good practice to engage in debate to clarify contentious issues that call into question the values espoused and their influence on the correctness of decisions. As an exercise in understanding oneself better, it would be beneficial to imagine scenarios that would put strain on the resolve to hold on to values, and to work out likely outcomes of such situations. The exercise may be painful at times, but it does get the mentor better prepared before such situations crop up unannounced.

There are a few cautions to be kept in mind for mentors in dealing with values. Discretion is a commodity to be liberally dispensed in imparting values to others. What is good for one may not necessarily be good for others. In this, it is not essential that the values that the mentor holds dear also be cherished as much by the mentee.

Then again, the mentor must also understand that there is a strong cultural basis to certain kinds of values being held dear. For example, certain cultures place an exceedingly high premium on honesty, while some do not value it as much. The importance attached to values like respect for elders, discipline, loyalty, and so on, is strongly influenced by cultural factors. In a culturally diverse country like India, the mentor's understanding of the nuances of how values are viewed becomes paramount to the success of mentoring. The differences may manifest themselves along the lines of variations in culture across geographic regions, along community or caste lines, across the generational divide, or as cross-gender differences.

It is a mutual call on whether the differences in values are so great that they are irreconcilable. If they are, then the question arises as to whether they interfere with the relationship and the process that both have embarked upon. If here too the issue is grave, then it would be extremely difficult for the process or the relationship to lead to any form of success.

In issues that have to do with values or are connected with them, it is recommended that the mentor leave the choice of whether the point of view should be accepted or otherwise to the mentee. But then, there can be no substitute for dialog in clarifying positions, reconciling differences and finding amicable solutions.

## ATTITUDE OF THE MENTOR

The mentor has taken on the mentee with the understanding that she/he would be helping the mentee progress in the profession and in life, and become a better person as a result. Having adopted the mentee, so to speak, the keenness of the mentor in seeing the development of the mentee is essential for the success of the process. It is this outlook that takes the relationship and the process forward.

That the mentor's attitude towards the process, the relationship and the mentee should be positive is something that does not even need to be iterated. That the mentor is well disposed towards the organization and the social system at large does form a significant contribution to the mentee feeling the positive vibes and imbibing a positive and bright outlook. After all, that is one of the desired outputs from the process.

The mentor is also to coach the mentee in the ways of the world, the profession and the organization. Being a coach in this respect, the mentor has to take the mentee for what she/he is and work towards giving the best and getting the best out of the mentee. It may at times happen that the mentee turns out to become better than the mentor herself/himself. This should actually be a matter of pride for the mentor and should not evoke a sense of insecurity. Clearly, the mentor should not be in competition with the mentee, and adequate care should be taken in ensuring that this is understood by both. Beyond mere understanding, there is a need for belief and conviction in this regard.

The position that the mentor must have in mind is that the entire effort is for the good of the system, the organization and society. This has to be the focus in all matters and activities in the process. There may be instances where there is a temptation to focus on one's own benefit, or that of the mentee, over the larger good of the system. But then, that is where the maturity of the mentor comes in to thwart the temptation and enables her/him to take the correct path. Further, there may be situations where there is a conflict between the interests of the system and those of the mentee. In this case, it is the mentor's discretion on which side to favor. This dilemma is a difficult situation to be in, as there is the responsibility of having adopted the mentee on the one hand, while on the other lies the responsibility of protecting the interests of the system.

One of the difficult ideas to adjust to for most mentors initially is that there are no material rewards, and the fulfilment in the process comes from the celebration of the mentee's successes in life. Investing in the mentee without a thought for ROI (return on investment) is a challenging matter in this world, tied as it is to material gratifications. Further, one is making the investment in a mentee without a bound commitment to reciprocate in the manner that she/he gains from the process. It takes some reconfiguring of attitudes to adjust to this.

## WIIFM

The mentor must be clear about the reasons why she/he is in the process and the relationship. It is the 'WIIFM' (What's In It For Me) that actually guides the actions of the mentor during the process. A wrong step here and the mentor could find herself/himself wide of the target when it comes to success in mentoring. This clarity is essential for the mentor to focus on building the relationship and work towards in helping the mentee through the process of development. To ensure this, it will be good if the mentor gets a fix on some of these aspects of herself/himself.

As a mentor, first try and figure out what drives you. What is it that gives you a feeling of elation, of being on top of the world? What activity, pursuit or prize makes you give your best to achieve? What aspect of your life do you treasure most and would like to build up further?

Second, be clear about your own personal and professional goals. Where are you headed? What do you intend to achieve in your profession and career? Get a measure of how far have you got in these matters and how much further you need to go. What are the issues or challenges you need to face?

Third, be as clear as you can about your needs. Needs can come in different forms: material, emotional, psychological, physical, sexual, aesthetic, social, economic, etc. How capable are you of providing for them or meeting them yourself, without aid from other quarters?

Fourth, are you geared to take up additional responsibility and the weight of another person looking up to you? How dependent are you on others? What are your dependencies? How are you dealing with them, if you are aware of them?

When you have as much clarity on these issues as you can get, you will know what you are into mentoring for. Thereafter, it is your own responsibility to check on the legitimacy of the reason and how it relates to mentoring. Please remember, what you are doing does not become mentoring just by calling it that.

Here are some of the WIIFMs that mentors often discover about themselves. Some are positive and the others are not. It is for each to work out how they have to be dealt with.

| The positive WIIFMs | The not-so-positive WIIFMs |
|---|---|
| Learning | Power |
| Helping | Control |
| Sharing | Information |
| Feeling energetic | Sponsoring |
| Belonging | Reliving youth |
| Teaching | Appreciation |
| Giving back to society | |
| Helping the underprivileged | |
| Way of life | |
| Nothing at all | |

| And a few WIIFMs that are both | |
|---|---|
| | Networking |
| | Recognition |
| | Relationship |

## MATURITY AND WISDOM

Long years of experience and practice in the profession (and in life) leave a positive mark. This is the reason why a mentor is valued so highly. The mentor has the benefit of having nothing to prove to anybody as such. She/he is secure in this feeling, and with herself/himself.

The many years of experience and the ability to look beyond the immediate experience helps conceptualize the world around and view things fairly objectively. The ability to detach oneself from events and look at them, analyzing the issues dispassionately, is the hallmark of a mentor. The low need for control and uncompromisingly high personal standards help in taking a philosophical view of the world. Generally unruffled and, in a sense, unexcitable, the mentor is able to remain calm in the most tumultuous situations.

The wisdom and maturity also go a long way towards equipping the mentor to be able to handle ambiguities in life and situations. There are circumstances and settings where there may be shades of gray, and things may be neither black nor white. Not everything is clearly defined and there may be times when contradictions emerge. Such situations are most likely in dealing with people and their lives.

In these situations the ability to understand divergent perspectives on the same issue, the apparent correctness of contradictory approaches and how to reconcile them without creating conflicts and discord is something that the mentor must also be capable of. The wisdom to hold unlikely companions—in ideas, thoughts, feelings, and people—together and still maintain the peace is a mentor's gift.

Mentors must also have the maturity to be conscious of not trying to relive their own lives or their missed years through the experiences and lives of the mentees. This is a vital aspect of mentoring. Understanding this and paying heed to this aspect governs the success of the relationship and leaves the mentee feeling good about the experience of the process.

## THE INDIAN ETHOS AND MENTORING

Working in an Indian environment has its charms. Indian civilization and culture have a recorded history of almost 5,000 years. A history as long and rich as this is bound to influence the present, in subtle and not-so-subtle ways. The legacy of the past 5,000 years cannot be set aside or wished away as unsuitable in a 'modern' industrial and information age. The soothing and comforting security of the glorious past has its own means of finding its way into the inner recesses of the Indian mentor's mind.

Practices, expectations and beliefs in Indian organizations are fairly strongly influenced by traditional Indian values. This traditionalism in the organization manifests itself in the relationship between people in different forms. The manifested aspects are in three broad groups of expectations and relationship behaviors: paternalism, patronage, and familial identity.

Not being mutually exclusive, they overlap, run concurrently or form a matrix in their manifestations in the organization. They rise out of people's expectations that are a throwback to mores of the past. They are influences in the Indian environment that affect both the mentor and the mentee. The degree of influence may vary, depending on factors like the socialization and background of the individual, the organizational environment, age, etc.

## Paternalism

Paternalism as an institution is perhaps the extension of the joint family system in India, where the *karta* is the head of the joint family organization. The approaches and practices of the *karta* are on the lines of paternalism. He is the father figure and the source of all collective security, authority, and strength.

Paternalism appears to be the cornerstone of Indian social and cultural organizations, and, by extension, in some form or the other, in Indian industrial organizations too. Tied to paternalism are such traits as familial identity, a sense of security, respect for seniority and age, the importance of the personality of the leader, unconditional obedience of authority, and patronage.

The institution (organization), like the joint family in the social environment, is important in paternalism, and nothing is done that is detrimental to it. The practice of paternalism in the organization takes the form of the leaders or heads of departments, divisions or regions taking on the roles of father figures towards the people working under them.

Paternalism does not bestow advantages or gratification in any form that is unfavorable to the culture and norms of the system. As a father figure, the informal *karta* takes an active interest in the development and growth of the people. Paternalism, in a sense, goes well with the role of the mentor.

There is however, also a downside to paternalism. Paternalism is very tolerant and accommodative of the less-than-adequate capabilities of the people who 'belong.' Like in a joint family, all who belong are taken care of, irrespective of the extent of capability or contribution to the output of the system. This does not work well at all in a competitive environment and in organizations keen on being lean and not carrying the burden of less productive passengers.

Paternalism does not necessarily conform to the formal structures in the organization, although they usually run parallel to each other. In paternalism, the center of power is singular, and there is no rivalry, with everyone knowing her/his place. The presence of rivalry or dual centers of power gives rise to the system of patronage, which is quite distinct from the system of paternalism.

## Patronage

The system of patronage is internecine and is based on the principle of the individual aligning relationships in the system to achieve her/his own ends. While not always to the detriment of the organization, it could, in a sense, affect the motivation of the people, in that it could divide the organization into different cliques and camps. Consequently, it could affect cohesion in the organization.

Patronage is sometimes called the 'godfather culture.' The patron is the 'godfather,' who heads the clique and uses members within it to enhance her/his power and control. The patron dispenses her/his largesse to people who are members of her/his clique so as to retain their loyalty; the patron can also be virulent towards the members of rival cliques. The people who subscribe to this system are in it for the advantages that can be obtained for themselves, even if they are at the cost of the system. In the Indian social environment, this manifests itself as the feudal culture of yore.

There is, however, some strength in the system of patronage. While patronage is not the best thing for the organization, it ensures the continuity and perpetuation of the organization. Once infected, the organization may weaken over time, but is kept alive because without it patronage comes to an end as well.

In present-day Indian industry and management, patronage is a congenital malady. Thriving on the expectations of paternalism ingrained in the social and cultural mores of the people, it takes root easily.

## Familial identity

Paternalism and patronage systems are both closely linked to family traditions in India, and are akin to the norms and practices that have evolved over the centuries in the familial setting in India.

Familial expectations spread beyond blood and consanguineous relationships to encompass all individuals working in the organization. This form of expectation comes from the socio-cultural environment and pervades the entire organization. New entrants into the organization go through subtle initiation and 'socialization' to gain acceptability in groups and the organization.

Socialization into groups helps establish understanding and commonality. It also incorporates new entrants into the group or organizational belief system. It offers them the warmth of belonging and the security of being taken care of. This is often sought in organizations where the people have long tenures.

The family as the center of life is not peculiar to India alone—this system exists in all agrarian societies, even those that are in the process of shedding agrarianism in favor of the 'modern' industrial culture. The agrarian way of life over the past few thousand years has given rise to the social structure based on the family as the basic unit.

It is not that traditionalism does not exist or is not practiced in other countries and regions. Each culture that has a long social history evolves its own form or variation of traditionalism. Family-centric behavior, which appears to be the manifest expression of traditionalism in most societies that have risen from the agrarian way of life, may in turn find its way into organizations and organizational life.

As a mentor, there is much that must be understood not only about oneself but also about the environment around. The constant exploration of one's own mind and the dynamics of culture keeps the mentor from tripping over unseen issues or being caught unprepared. For this, keeping the mentor's mind sharp is an added responsibility.

# 5

# MENTORING COMPETENCIES AND SKILLS

'MENTORS are highly skilled people.' That sounds nice and rings true. These are, after all, people we would like to admire and look up to. They would be, we take it, people with an exceptional wealth of qualities we would like in ourselves.

But the reality is that this may by no means be wholly true. Mentors can be very ordinary people with ordinary skills and capabilities, normal levels of achievements and successes, and almost forgettable levels of particular skills and expertise.

The uniqueness of a great mentor is that for the mentee the 'chemistry' falls so perfectly in place that there is nothing further she/he needs to look for. The 'perfect fit' does not require superlatives in everything or an exceptional high in some areas, but needs only to have acceptable or required base-level competencies and skills to work out well for the mentee in that particular window in time. This is not a demanding calling.

What the 'acceptable' or the 'required base-level' of competencies and skills is cannot be generalized to meet a 'mentoring' calibration, but would be governed by the factors that govern the success of the mentoring process. So it would be prudent not to compare one mentor with another. There are several factors that matter.

Let us take a look at some of the factors: the organic organizational environment; the level of technology and the technological environment; the field or area the mentor or the mentee work in; the intellectual levels and requirements of the mentor and the mentee; the expectations of the mentor and the mentee; the benchmarks that the mentor and the mentee have experienced or encountered and have hence set for themselves; the criteria of success as mutually defined; the organizational and peer-level expectations; the image and reputation the mentor and the mentee command; and so on.

Whatever these factors, mentors need to aspire to and develop adequate skills and competencies in some areas, and have attitudes conducive to the process to achieve any measure of success or measure up to the expectations of mentees. These areas include:

1. Investment in learning and development
2. Success orientation
3. Altruism
4. Heightened self-awareness
5. Technical expertize in the chosen field
6. Focused approach/goal clarity
7. Communication skills
8. Empathy and sensitivity
9. Relationship skills
10. Conceptualization skills

All these, when present in the required measure, help the mentor rise from good to great. Of these qualities, the individual may have a core depth that is greater in one as compared to others; but not having one or more of these may leave the mentee feeling inadequate in the process.

Let us first consider the attributes. Attributes are qualities associated with the persons, their characteristic qualities, something that is an integral/innate part of them. Mentors have to have some basic indispensable attributes.

## INVESTMENT IN LEARNING AND DEVELOPMENT

This is an attribute on which there can be no compromise; which is absolutely necessary in a mentor. The right orientation and leaning towards learning and development would certainly make the mentor invaluable to the mentee and, by extension, to the organization or the social system they are a part of. The baseline objective of the mentoring process is itself learning and individual development.

A mentor with humility—the humility to learn—is among the best of her/his kind. The humility that comes with the belief that any one of us—and, more important, oneself—can be a learner is a core attribute in a mentor. This attribute sets the context of the relationship, the nature and success of mentoring. This humility would facilitate the establishment of unbridled openness and the ability of the mentor and the mentee to accept each other for what they are.

The mentor has to accord a particularly high priority to learning as a part of the professional and life process. The primary task of the mentor is to create learning opportunities for the mentee, to help widen the mentee's mental horizons (as well as the mentor's own), and to encourage efforts in learning and development. The mentor must also be one who appreciates skill and knowledge gained in any form by the mentee.

Further, the investment put into learning and development would keep the relationship in the right frame and prevent it from slipping into undesirable and unintended areas. The growth and maturity of the mentee is faster and better if there is greater investment in learning and development.

---

**Case study 5.1** | Wringing out the best

Lalitha Iyengar's coffee had gone cold, and my coke had gone flat, but that did not matter. Here was a lesson I was getting an opportunity to imbibe that I could not have got anywhere else. It was certainly worth more than the coke or the great coffee that I was told was served in the corporate office here. I had left the coke and noticed that Lalitha had left her coffee.

The young girl was sitting in the chair across the room, sobbing uncontrollably. She could barely get her words of desperation out coherently. Lalitha had moved over from behind the huge desk and sat in the chair across from the young girl. She let the girl's extreme emotion and her outburst run its course. She then offered her a box of face tissues.

The girl had burst in suddenly into the room where I had a meeting with Ms. Lalitha Iyengar, the Deputy Director (Finance). The girl paid little heed to me but started venting her rage on Lalitha before breaking into uncontrollable sobs. All that Lalitha said at that time was, 'Jayanthi, sit down,' as she moved around the desk to reach the girl. Lalitha had nodded and smiled her apology to me and I too had silently nodded.

CONTINUED ON THE NEXT PAGE

CASE STUDY 5.1—CONTINUED

The burden of Jayanthi's grouse against Lalitha Iyengar was that she had always saddled Jayanthi with projects that were very difficult and required the hardest work. She had always been the one chosen for doing assignments requiring traveling and interfacing with difficult people in other departments. She had to stay back late quite often, and still found she was behind schedule all the time. While she was being 'harassed' in such a manner, the other people in her grade and her colleagues in other departments were 'enjoying' life in the company. Lalitha was the worst boss anyone could have. (She didn't actually say the last sentence, but the message couldn't have been clearer.) If I didn't know Lalitha Iyengar, from the tirade that had been delivered against her I would have believed her to be an ogre and a slave driver.

'Jayanthi,' Lalitha said calmly after Jayanthi had regained a semblance of control, 'the only difference between what you are saying about your first boss and what I had said about my first boss is that I had played this scene out almost 25 years before you did.

'Yes, almost 25 years ago, I too had barged into my boss's room and charged him with almost the same things you have accused me of today, the only difference being that I did not interrupt any meeting,' Lalitha said, smiling. 'I was about your age then and I saw the world the same way you do now. And I will tell you what my boss told me then. It is still very clear in my mind and I don't think I can ever forget that lesson.

'He had told me that he was certainly being partial and biased in his dealings with me when compared with how other bosses work with their subordinates. "The others

CONTINUED ON THE NEXT PAGE

get all the easy jobs, the ones that require less work. But you will get all the difficult ones, the ones that challenge you. You will find yourself run down by the end of the day and so tired that you will find it hard to even sleep."

'"But," he told me, "there is a motive in what I am getting you to do. One, that you will get better with each challenge, since you will not learn to make the extra effort unless you feel the pressure. Second, that every opportunity you come across is a fresh learning opportunity, not a repeat of the old and comfortable. Third, you keep on with this and you will learn to meet each challenge and learn to win each time. Learning and winning becomes a habit. While others get comfortable with the common jobs, you have the opportunity to become exceptional."

'That was 25 years ago. Today I am Deputy Director and my former colleagues are still working their way past Senior Manager. Today I see the wisdom of what my first boss had put me through.

'So, Jayanthi,' Lalitha Iyengar continued, 'As long as you are with me, I will work you so hard that your fingers may fall off, give you the most difficult and challenging tasks, put you through the hardest work. But I am sure that I will get an outstanding Jayanthi out of this rather than a pedestrian Jayanthi.

'If you want the comfort of the ordinary, you will not create learning opportunities, but if you are willing to extend yourself, each step will give you new learning and growth—maybe not immediately, but it will come. If you work with me, I can promise you that I will drive you and make you grow. But if you choose to take the slow and easy road, you will be spending a long time on the road before you get to where you want to reach. You decide, Jayanthi.'

CONTINUED ON THE NEXT PAGE

Jayanthi, poor girl, had no words left to say. She quietly rose and left the room.

I did not return to check on which road Jayanthi chose to travel on, but there was much that I could pick up from what happened that day in Lalitha Iyengar's room. Lalitha Iyengar is today also one of the most popular and successful mentors in that company.

## SUCCESS ORIENTATION

The mentor must have a positive orientation towards succeeding in projects and activities she/he takes up. This should not just be in terms of polemical statements like 'Nobody begins with the thinking she/he will fail,' but in having the zeal to go for success as if that is the whole purpose in taking up the project. This fundamental belief is in itself an essential component.

A belief in oneself; a good measure of understanding of one's capabilities; a mind rooted to reality and practical possibilities; willingness to run the gauntlet in giving what it takes to get things done; and the desire to give it your best shot are the features of this attribute. An attribute such as this cannot lie hidden. It also acts as a positive contagion, getting into those who come into contact with the person.

For the mentee there can be little that is more important than being able to bask in this positive energy and imbibe it. If she/he can replicate it in herself/himself, there is so much to be gained in the process. The mentor cultivates this milieu around herself/himself, and the mentee has so much to absorb from this environment and the mentor who maintains it.

## ALTRUISM

Consider Mother Teresa's words: 'Give till it hurts.' This may be a bit excessive in this context, and is hardly to be expected in the environment of acquisitiveness and materialism in the corporate world, but somewhere in these words is a message that should strike a chord in the mentor's mind. Certainly the mentor is neither expected to be nor needs to be a philanthropist. But a measure of unselfishness does find a strong place in the repertoire of the mentor's positive attributes.

Wanting to help others is a fine quality, but wanting to help without expectation of reward is better still. A mentor's approach to her/his mission is very much on these lines. The satisfaction and eventually the energy that the mentor derives in the success of her/his mentee is in itself a prize. She/he is happy to share achievements and successes with others whom she/he is trying to bring up in the profession and life.

A basic level of this attribute is necessary in the mentor for her/him to be successful in mentoring. Also, the caution is to not get carried away in making mentoring a philanthropic activity. Mentoring has a specific focus, purpose and meaning; it is not a general do-good, bleeding-heart charity. In understanding where to draw the line lies the wisdom of the mentor.

## HEIGHTENED SELF-AWARENESS

There are issues which people live with—some people have a few, some have several. In dealing with others, clarity about the issues that confront each of us is important, particularly because the risk of the mentors' own issues warping their approach to mentees' issues is very real.

The mentor's awareness—not only of the issues she/he is grappling with on her/his own account, but also the strengths and liabilities, the limitations and capabilities—is quite essential in becoming a good and competent mentor.

A good way to heighten self-awareness is a constant self-exploration and examination of one's own experiences, behaviors and responses to many things: relationships, circumstances and the world outside. One must allow each experience to be a learning step, each incident an indicator to glean insights into oneself. To be able to get a good and composite picture of the kind of person one is would definitely be an invaluable asset that can be leveraged in mentoring.

Having a counselor or a confidante who could hold up a mirror to facilitate an objective look at oneself is also an efficient means of heightening self-awareness. Accessing a counselor or confidante—if not regularly, at least periodically—could definitely clear the mental and emotional cobwebs that might fog the glass through which one pictures oneself. This could also have a spin-off in better understanding the client–counselor relationship.

Awareness of the capabilities and competencies, troubles and travails that reside within oneself is the essential first step in dealing with and sorting out the internal psychological blocks and barriers of others. This leads progressively to greater preparedness in dealing with other people's issues and helping them to deal with them and find a solution.

A good mentor is on a constant journey of self-exploration, and each discovery adds to the resources that can increase her/his competency in mentoring. Being aware of oneself also gives a good measure of the impact one has on others, the influence one bears on the relationship and also the reciprocal influence of others on oneself. Awareness is a good first step towards the prudent management and control of relationships.

## TECHNICAL EXPERTISE IN THE CHOSEN FIELD

The mentor should ideally be a respected person in the chosen field. Technical expertise and standing adds much to the stature and credibility of the individual. Constant striving to be in the vanguard of the area of core interest and work is an ability much valued in the mentor. This is definitely one aspect that gains almost instant admiration and respect when coupled with other attributes and skills.

Since one of the core objectives of mentoring is the provision of guidance and perspectives to the mentee, it is a desired competency for the mentor to be an expert in the area, preferably in a position commanding admiration.

Supplementing this are experience and perspective in management, usually at the senior levels, that the mentor can bring in to add value to the process. If the mentor has worked in different organizations, this also helps widens the horizons of the mentee. The mentor's insights in studying management or related fields; the consulting experience or exposure that the mentor may have; the cross-functional experience and understanding; the depth in thinking about everyday issues in managing in the organizational context—all these contribute to the value of the process.

Further, the technical expertise in the mentor's chosen field is built over long years in the practice of the profession; the wide reading that the mentor would have undertaken; the good professional networks that have been established; and a good command of the current thinking in the field. This actually works out in quite a few cases as being the core competency of the mentor.

## FOCUSED APPROACH/GOAL CLARITY

Being success-oriented is one thing, but carrying it to an appropriate level and ensuring that the right things happen at the right time and in the right sequence requires clarity about the goals and targets.

Being clear about what any project, activity or initiative is driving towards adds greatly to its chances of success. Breaking the goal down to each achievable detail, systematizing the approach and plan of work, and understanding the nuances of each aspect is a great competency to have in a mentor. The ability to visualize and to then pre-empt the possibility of any unforeseen occurrence is a fairly valuable asset.

Being single-minded and focused on the set objective, giving it all and working towards the singular objective of success in the quest is a grand competency to have under the mentor's belt. One of the essential and crucial competencies that the mentor can transfer to the mentee is to clarify and be certain of the goal, and be focused in striving towards it.

Achieving goal clarity and focus requires the basic and innate ability to be able to perceive the larger picture while not sacrificing the ability to keep the details in view as well. The mentor should have the ability to rise above the immediate and distracting issues and put the main problem, issue or work in perspective. She/he should be able to discern the impact this might have on connected or neighboring issues; to delineate the impinging issues that drag themselves in with the main issue; to capture the ramifications of taking different courses towards the solution; and to judge which could be the best course or approach should be taken under that particular situation or circumstance.

All these need to be combined with this the ability to work single-mindedly and to bring all attention and energy to bear on the immediate task at hand, without being distracted by preoccupations of whatever intensity that divert attention from the task or issue that one is engaged in. Cultivating this competency through perseverance and practice would earn the mentor rich dividends.

| Case study 5.2 | Never let anything beat you! |

For Ashok Razdan it wasn't about attitude or outlook ... it was plain lifestyle. There was no other way he had led his life. Life had just one purpose for him: to get the job done! For him, no target came with a disclaimer clause regarding why it could not be met. For as long as he could remember, this was the way he had led his life and he knew no other way.

But now something else was happening. These young boys were telling him something different, and he sat there listening. These young executives in his Business Unit were

CONTINUED ON THE NEXT PAGE

all speaking in one voice, almost as if they had the statement all rehearsed. He let them continue.

It had been going on for over 20 minutes now. Slowly the tempo flagged, and gradually it began dawning on the executives that Razdan wasn't buying it. A few lapsed into silence, but the others persisted. Razdan let them go on.

Finally they too paused and they all turned towards Razdan. Some looked down, some still held his gaze, not defiant but hopeful that their frantic filibuster would have held back Razdan from pushing through what appeared to them to be a suicidal target.

Razdan regarded them with a steady gaze and a wry smile. He knew each one very well. He had studied them all thoroughly over the past year. They were all hardy youngsters who had put in some hard time in the extremely competitive and ruthless field of direct sales. They had fought through and stayed in this tough environment. Their word would have been considered seriously anywhere.

'When I say that I have assured the CEO and the MC (Management Committee) that our BU will hit Rs 430 crores the coming year, by God we will hit 430. Not 400, not 420, not 429–430 it will have to be! Yes, it is a 40 percent rise over last year, but the market itself is growing at 30 percent.' Beginning in this manner, Razdan spoke continuously for 25 minutes.

'It is not a matter of what you can do, but what you believe you can do. The figure 430 appears to terrorize you, but you also need to look at yourselves. We have beaten the target each quarter last year and each time it has been more than 25 percent over the previous one.

'Take a look at what you felt when you had licked the target each time!

CONTINUED ON THE NEXT PAGE

CASE STUDY 5.2—CONTINUED

'From the time I've been your age, I've always worked to see how much more I can do, how much further I can stretch myself. That's how I've grown to what I am today.

'I've never let anybody get the better of me. You shouldn't let that happen to you either.

'The most important thing here is that 430 is not a target I want. It is not a target that the CEO or the MC wants. It's a target that I think you can beat. I have the faith—not in the market, not in luck, but in you. I'm there to work with you, and let's not give up before trying. Let's go for it! I am standing by you. Let's beat the sh** out of 430 and show them!'

This was an incident that took place three years ago. Today Ashok Razdan is Director of the company and a Member of the MC. His drive and energy is just as high today. It is his infectious enthusiasm that has transformed so many others in the company into great successes.

## COMMUNICATION SKILLS

Communication is not a single skill in itself. It is a cluster of skills that focus on dealing successfully and efficiently with messages and information. It covers a range of skills. Some may be integral and contribute to the efficiency in the way messages and transactions are dealt with by the mentor and the mentee.

Significant for the mentor is the skill of listening and then being able to articulate her/his mind to the mentee. Listening itself comprises capturing what is being said and also being able to discern what has not been said. Articulation involves skill at handling language and using the trans-verbal—non-verbal and para-verbal—aspects of communication as well.

The mentor has to be a good listener in the first place. There is no substitute for this, and a skill such as this is among the most effective in leading the mentor to success in her/his efforts.

Listening does not imply being a passive and inactive recipient. Listening is an 'active' activity. It involves in itself a repertoire of subtle skills.

First comes patience. The mentor is a patient person, not hurried and restless, impatient and intolerant about letting the mentee take time in getting the message across. Patience in good measure is essential to help the mentee ease up and find comfort in relating and then communicating with the mentor. This would ensure that the mentee does not feel pushed into finishing quickly, leaving a feeling of desperation, frustration, and inadequacy.

Patience comes with the understanding that communication is not your show entirely but that you are a recipient in the process. As a recipient your success depends on the encouragement that you can give to the person who is delivering the message to you. Patience is, on the one hand, not being restless, wanting to move ahead without pausing for the others to catch up; and on the other it involves being able to control or keep the restlessness from showing itself and interfering with the process.

This requires awareness and clarity about the cues and subtle messages that tend to show up the restlessness within. While not being impatient when dealing with the mentee is the best, the other option is to be careful to not let the restiveness within disturb the mentee in her/his attempt at communicating. As a listener, this is a prime responsibility.

In addition to receiving the message, being an 'active listener' involves registering the message and also providing some form of feedback as a participant in the communication loop. Providing some form of appropriate feedback, especially as quick and silent non-verbal cues or small verbal ones, not only serves as an indicator of attention being paid to the speaker but also indicates the fact that the message is being registered. Coming from a mentor, this adds to the comfort in the relationship with the mentee.

Listening also involves an important and crucial aspect of observing the cues that accompany the speaking, and reading the meaning in these cues. This, in a sense, is visual listening. It requires going beyond merely what is said and capturing the whole message. There is often a lot of hidden meaning and silent messages that escort the main vocal message. Grasping these quiet accessories to the main message is a particular skill that is part of being a good communicator. This is one aspect that the mentor must concentrate on.

In articulating her/his thoughts and ideas to the mentee, the mentor's proficiency is most crucial. For one, having good articulation skills is a widely admired quality. This is also one skill that the mentor must get the mentee to imbibe and develop.

In articulation, there is the verbal component and the trans-verbal one. The verbal component has to do with the way the language system is used to convey meaning. This is the most consciously transacted part of communication.

Proficiency in this aspect depends on the two main parts of the way language is put to use: the command of the language, and its usage. Command of the language is the extent of control the user has over the language, i.e., the number of words at her/his command, the vocabulary. In broad terms, the larger the vocabulary, the more maneuverable and malleable the language is in the hands of the user. Working at extending the vocabulary in the particular language is crucial for greater clarity and accuracy in expression.

And then there is the usage of the language. The usage of the language involves the grammatical and syntactical norms of the language—essentially how the words in a language are strung together to convey a meaningful message. In any language, the rules governing the usage of the language also govern the way the language is understood.

In the verbal part, the ease and fluency that the mentor has with the language is significant. What the language is may not be as important as how it is used. The ability to articulate in the language understood by the mentee; using examples, clichés, and metaphors to illustrate; and cutting jargon down to the level of the mentee are equally important in the verbal skill. This extends as much to the oral as to the written format of usage.

Going beyond verbal proficiency is the huge trans-verbal part of communication. The trans-verbal component comprises para-verbal communication and non-verbal communication. The para-verbal components are the non-language parts of verbal communication, like intonation, accent, emphasis, pronunciation, use of silence, gestures supplementing the spoken word, etc. Understanding them and putting them to correct use makes for greater efficiency in communication.

The non-verbal part is the much larger part of the transaction of meaning. This is the non-standardized component of the transaction and includes the use of gestures (body language, kinesics), time, space, social codes, graphics, color, dress, adornments, etc. This is a complex and intricate part of communication. It is closely bound to the culture, situation and context of communication. That over 95 percent of the non-verbal communication occurs without the individual consciously knowing about it actually makes this kind of communication a leakage of information. By capturing these leakages, one can in fact know more about a person than she/he intends to communicate. Learning to use, understand and be proficient in this is extremely useful. For with this, the mentor has the capability not only to transact what she/he intends, but also to understand the mentee beyond what the mentee may communicate verbally.

As a communicator, the mentor must not only have the skill but also a consciousness of the process so as to ensure that the communication with the mentee is a two-way transaction. Feedback is as vital to communication as feed-forward. The responsiveness to create avenues and channels for feedback is the hallmark of a good communicator.

Also, as a part of the repertoire of skills called communication is the ability to excite and enthuse the mentee into communicating openly, and being able to ask insightful and, at times, searching questions. A set of skills such as this is an essential prerequisite for anybody venturing into the fold of mentoring.

## EMPATHY AND SENSITIVITY

This skill forms one of the main pillars of any human relations process. Mentoring is primarily a human relations process. Dealing with any person requires understanding her/him and taking the relationship forward from there. Empathy and sensitivity are skills that ensure success in this.

Empathy is the ability to put oneself in the other person's position and see the issue, context and subject in the way the other person sees it. It is the ability to look beyond one's own issues and understand the perspectives of the other. A cosmopolitan outlook; an understanding of a wide array of concerns; being aware of different perspectives on issues; an intimate knowledge and understanding of the mentee; keenness in observing and capturing the nuances in communication; and an ardent interest in the mentee's development would all provide a good foundation to augment this skill and make it workable for the mentor.

Sensitivity is the ability to discern the emotions and feelings of the other without them necessarily being articulated. This skill bestows on the mentor the ability to read the mentee well and understand her/him beyond her/his capability to express herself/himself. It increases the care and concern that the mentor can offer the mentee in trying times.

## RELATIONSHIP SKILLS

Relationship skills have to do with the ability to build, maintain and carry forward relationships with a measure of success. Relationships between people have delicate facets and subtle nuances about them that need great care and sharpness to understand and working with. To quite a few, this is an innate ability; for others it is a learned art; and for a few it is something quite out of their grasp. The thing to understand is that when building a relationship an entity called the relationship itself gets created and this has demands of its own. Managing this is the significant part.

For the mentor this is a critical skill, as mentoring is directly a people and relationship activity. The ability and skill to build, handle and manage relationships is a part of being a mentor. Primary in this is the knack of keeping the interest and the energy levels high within the relationship. The ability to get both to mutually invest in the relationship and maximize and harness the synergy that exudes from it governs the strength of the relationship.

The skills include understanding the dynamics in the relationship; balancing the contributions and takeaways from it; detecting and seizing opportunities to strengthen it; identifying the needs of the relationship and the participants; negotiating positions and issues between participants; and pre-empting, resolving, and managing conflicts. There is much the mentor can do towards keeping the relationship with the mentee on an even keel and working out the best that can be had from it.

Any relationship is a shared enterprise. It has to be mutually nurtured. The skill in relationship building has to be imbibed by both participants, and a good negotiated understanding on how it should be maintained needs to be shared. There is no substitute for constant housekeeping to maintain the relationship in good health.

There may also be relationships that can move into being one-sided, where one is contributing to and nurturing the relationship more while the other is making a lesser or no contribution. If the need for the relationship is high on one side, then the negotiated terms may be tipping heavily towards that side. The future of such relationships is not too bright when the need no longer exists. It is depends on each individual how she/he intends to negotiate her/his share in the relationship. This aspect is a skill in itself.

## CONCEPTUALIZATION SKILLS

This is one skill that normally lurks along the fringes, but is in the case of the mentor crucial to the work she/he has taken on. This is the ability to put things in perspective, and evolve a pattern and concept out of the clutter of happenings, issues, information, behaviors, etc. This has a very strong foundation in the ability to hold together a large number of divergent aspects of various things and see patterns and commonalities in them, to put them in some form of order, and in a sense create a concept out of them. This makes for approaching similar or comparable situations with better preparedness and familiarity.

In large measure this comes from the maturity and sagacity that the mentor has. It helps the mentee understand and grasp the significance of apparently unconnected things. In the larger sense it helps the mentee lead a more fruitful life, understanding how the various pieces fit into the bigger picture.

Wider exposure to the ideas and thinking of people with this particular skill, keeping an open mind, having the curiosity and inquisitiveness to explore, and trying to working out the rationale behind happenings goes into building up this capability. It certainly helps to have a philosophical bent of mind here. This is one skill that takes long to acquire, but once acquired it is there to stay.

These are the 10 crucial attributes, competencies and skills of the mentor. There are several more that can add to making the mentor that much better at the mission. Each new talent and capability that the mentor opens herself/himself out to adds value to the mentee as well. So it augurs well for the mentor to constantly explore and create opportunities for acquiring a wider array of capabilities to enhance personal effectiveness.

# 6

# ISSUES IN MENTORING

A relationship and practice such as mentoring throws up a plethora of issues to be understood and worked out by all those involved in it. Some of these issues are contentious and naggingly persistent, while others are insignificant enough to be ignored. But which of these impacts any particular relationship is hard to foretell. It is always prudent for any mentor—or mentee, for that matter—to be aware of and have spent time in considering them before they actually come visiting.

## ONE'S OWN CAREER AND SURVIVAL

There are ideal mentors and then there are mentors. Ideally the mentor is successful in her/his own right. She/he has built up life and career on the capabilities developed over time and with perseverance. The success and achievements of the mentor are something that she/he richly deserves.

This being the case, there would be not much of a problem in issues related to the mentor's own career in the profession and her/his continuance in the organizational scheme of things. However, there may be concerns with some mentors that are better addressed than left unattended.

Where a mentor has moved into mentoring following a successful career, she/he would be secure with the prospects and the growth that she/he can look forward to. Here the mentee is secure too, as she/he is not affected by the pre-occupations of the mentor with her/his own career. On the other hand, where the mentor is one who does not have a stream of successes behind her/him, what is important is how she/he views her/his own future. Not having a long successful record does not necessarily disqualify the person from being a mentor if the other competencies and capabilities, along with the spirit to work in this direction, are in place.

There would certainly be instances in every person's life where failures or incomplete successes are a part. The mentor deals with these instances in her/his life quite differently. The mentor should have been able to understand and rationalize the failure and the disappointment that may accompany it. She/he would have come to terms with the fallouts and not let them hold up or deter the progress or growth from there on. If the mentor has been able to work this out for herself/himself, the chances are good that she/he will be able to share these experiences with the mentee and also get the mentee to learn to handle the fallouts of falling short of success.

The mentor wears about her/him an air of contentment and satisfaction with regard to the achievements and progress in her/his career and future. This satisfaction is not born out of resignation to the inevitable, but is the contentment that comes from satisfactory movement towards a projected goal. While the mentor may be aggressively bullish about helping the mentee achieve her/his goals, she/he would be in a position to be more relaxed about her/his own goals.

In organizations that are fast-paced and forceful, there is often the chance of an internecine conflict slithering around the corner. This in all likelihood enfolds most people in its tight grip. Escaping its venomous coils is an art that is most valued by people who would like to keep a peaceful and stress-free environment for themselves. The mentor would be one who has mastered this art, and would have no part in the internecine quarrels in the organization. Even if they have been at times a part of such conflicts, it would be a thing of the past. This would leave the mentor free from having to constantly watch her/his own back.

For the mentor, professional respect would by far outweigh organizational standing. Being respected for what the mentor has achieved and acquired as knowledge and reputation is much more valuable for the mentor. The organizational dynamics of position and status holds little or no significance as such. Not that the mentor has signed out of the organizational systems, but she/he would be in a position to feel secure about where she/he stands. Then again, it is not that those deep in the organizational dynamics cannot be good mentors, but this may consume too much energy and would also leave the mentor entangled in too many issues.

The mentor is also clear about the societal and organizational values and her/his own personal values. The areas of conflict would have long ago been reconciled and are no longer irritants. The mentor should ideally be clear about not working against organizational or societal values that jeopardize the future of the mentee and perhaps warp her/his thinking and views. As a concept, this appears pretty easy to enunciate, but getting to this stage requires long years of working with and resolving issues that confound most people.

## POWER, AUTHORITY, AND HIERARCHY

Great mentors generally have a low need to control. They are willing to let people make up their own minds. They do not force their will on people; neither do they try the manipulative route. They are content to help people with perspectives, options, and advice. They are content to help people when help is sought. They are content to work with people in getting them out of difficulties they have landed themselves in. They are content with aiding people in making the right kind of decisions. But they do not try to control their decisions and actions.

This does not imply that they are passive bystanders to incidents and actions around them. By their very nature they are people whose views and ideas are respected and valued. They have a very high credibility and eminence in their world. Their advice is sought and valued enough to often be followed without question. This is their power. They have no urge to get others to do their bidding just because it is coming from them.

At the same time, they are quite happy with no authority in the system. They can get by quite comfortably without the burden of being constantly on the watch to guard their authority. They are often people with no outstanding conflicts with those in authority in the organization or the social system. They are very often non-interfering and non-threatening.

This appears pretty sedate and calm. The mentor is like this till the point of values and morals being transgressed. Past this threshold is when they would let loose the fury they are capable of. The enormity of their power is in their ability to draw on resources not easily seen and hence underestimated.

They have the humility of not flaunting their power. Theirs is the power of capability, of networking, of respect, of being held above ordinary people by others. They have no need to test their power and feel secure enough not to seek more of it.

Also, the mentor has a healthy respect for the system and structure in the organization and the social set-up. They would have rationalized their differences with the system and have come to terms with them. They are well aware of how the system works and do not consciously create conflicts that mar its smooth functioning.

This may make the mentor out to be someone less human and more of a *mahatma* (great soul). This is only an ideal, but the closer one can approach the ideal the better it would be in making a success of the mission one has embarked upon. It is a process of constant striving. Falling short on this score should not be a dampener and make people withdraw from the process. This is to give a measure of the heights one can aspire to reach.

## THE MENTOR AND THE LINE MANAGER

In the mentoring process the role of the line manager or the direct boss of the mentee is often underrated. This causes so many unseen and unexpected troubles and issues to surface when least called for. The line manager is an important stakeholder in the process and can make or break it. It would be a very good idea to keep her/him in the loop with respect to the inclusion of the mentee in the scheme.

There are huge advantages for the line manager in having the mentee go through the developmental process. There is a good likelihood of the mentee becoming better and more productive in the process. The line manager has access to a second opinion where that might be of help. Also, the line manager can either take the help of the mentor in the developmental interventions planned for the mentee or can offload much of the developmental responsibility on to the mentoring process.

At the same time, it must also be borne in mind that not all line managers will be as positively inclined to the mentoring effort as the mentor is. They can be skeptical and can ruin the good work being put in. Where this is a possibility, it will be good to sort the matter out before the interests of the mentee take a beating.

## MONEY

It is fairly normal for money to be an issue with everybody. It would be unrealistic to assume that for a mentor money or material acquisitions and comforts are not an issue. Money as such also represents a whole range of material aspects of life. Everybody needs money.

But the question here is of the priority one would attach to it. For a mentor, the ability to keep money-related issues outside the purview of the mentoring mission is important. She/he should have the maturity and the prudence to understand the turmoil that money issues can evoke in a relationship, particularly if the relationship is not firm and established enough to bear the strain.

How high a priority is money in the scheme of things for the mentor? And for the mentee? Does it, perhaps below the level of conscious thought, invade the time and mind space that has been booked for the mentoring activity? Do issues related to money in all its implications gain priority over the commitment to the mentee? Are issues of money such a matter of importance that learning and development take a back seat? Is there a tendency to measure all or most matters in terms of money? Is there a propensity to use money as a common denominator to match or equate things? These are issues that the mentor must clarify before embarking on the mission.

Having worked to achieve clarity on this, the mentor must heed this cardinal principle in mentoring. This is one of two vital principles. Here is the first (the second one, relating to gender issues, follows further on). Adopting this principle is a safeguard against the mentoring relationship getting vitiated or falling foul of the fundamentals of mentoring itself.

In a mentoring relationship, ideally leave money out of the equation. As is often said in life, so it should be mentoring too: neither a lender nor a borrower be. With the mentee, stick to this. To the furthest extent possible, try not to have any monetary transaction with the mentee. All too often in a relationship, when money-related transactions are involved, there is every likelihood of it veering off in a direction that may well be beyond the control of either the mentor or the mentee. This could very well work against the basic purpose of mentoring itself.

By all means, handling money and being prudent in its use is a skill that needs to be imparted to the mentee, and the independence and autonomy in the way money is dealt with are definitely important. But keeping money transactions between the mentor and mentee out of the picture is one of the most important and vital mutual understandings in the protocol that any mentor and mentee get into. It would also not be prudent to get into any form of business partnership with the mentee. If such a need arises, it is advisable to get a clear understanding and mutual protocol worked out well in advance.

## GENDER ISSUES IN MENTORING

Mentors of either sex have as much care to take when issues of gender come to the fore in mentoring. This is even truer when the mentee is on the other side of the gender divide.

Being sensitive to the subtle and different needs of the other gender is a built-in responsibility and comes with the package. The way women see issues of relationships and the requirements of younger people are subtly different from the way men do. This is more so with respect to the emotional aspects. However much there is a tendency to mask and ignore this, it does not go away.

There are important gender differences in the way feelings are expressed, the openness that is expected, the ability to handle ambiguity, the acknowledgment of differences, the acceptance of femininity, the choice of words and expressions, the difference in the use of language itself, the use of and reaction to humor, etc. There are differences, and the more sensitive the mentor is to these, the more comfortable the relationship will be. This comfort also governs the success of the mission in the relationship.

There is also a need for the mentor to be conscious of the gender issues in the social and professional setting. Each culture and community has its own set of issues and concerns when it comes to interaction between the sexes. These issues can be prevalent in the organization as well, particularly in organizations working in conservative and traditional environments. The mentor has to be conscious of this and at all times stay within the norms and expectations that govern accepted protocols. Any transgression should be out of a conscious effort and out of a mutually discussed and accepted need. The risk taken in such cases is something that may affect either, and hence it is essential to keep all decisions in this direction mutual.

The social prescription on how a relationship of mentoring is tenable across gender is often fairly clear in the way it may be stated. However, the mentor also has to be aware of the unstated aspects. While it may sometimes be good to argue in favor of social change with regard to points of view that may not be functional, it is always good to be aware and sure of what one is getting into and wanting to get into.

This brings us to the second cardinal principle in mentoring, the issue related to money being the other. The mentor and the mentee will, in all likelihood, work closely with one another. There is always a possibility of emotional and sexual entanglements developing. This is one area that should set off the alarm bells.

Relationships that have a different context and have started with other objectives tend to go off on a tangent when emotional and sexual attachments set in. The emotional and sexual context to relationships has a tendency to bring in the aspect of possessiveness, which is definitely not a healthy territory to move into in mentoring. The mentoring relationship also has to carry the burdens of other responsibilities when these entanglements find their way in. It often gets messier when the sentiment is only from one side and the other has to resist it. There can be any number of permutations and degrees of involvement, but the issue, except for the intensity, is similar.

The way around this is either to take the step of guarding against any such possibility and keep the relationship to the stated and agreed level, or to clearly get away from the mentoring relationship and work at the new context of the relationship. If the mentoring relationship is to endure, the protocol and context may have to be renegotiated and agreed upon. Whichever path is chosen, the prudent course is not to take any step or decision unilaterally.

## HITCHING YOUR WAGON TO THE MENTOR'S

How closely should the mentee tag her/his future to that of the mentor? Should the mentor carry the future of the mentee in her/his own hands? Where should the line be drawn?

This is a difficult question to give a specific answer to. The best is for the mentor and the mentee to take a mutually convenient position. The good thing to do would be to be open about this and come to a mutual understanding.

The mentee should not develop dependence to the extent of abdicating decision-making on her/his future into the hands of the mentor; this is something that the mentor must guard against. The mentee must remember that the mentor does not expect her/him to cross the gray line between deference and respect, and obedience and subservience. Being open to each other about this can be helpful in terms of providing support to each other.

It is also to be kept in mind that hitching the future of the mentee to the prospects of the mentor does limit the mentee to what the mentor can aspire to. While a mentor can be a role model, she/he need not be a benchmark. In the organizational context, too close an identification with the mentor has its own advantages and downsides. While sharing in celebrations and good times is a pleasant experience, the close identity with the mentor becomes a severe liability when the mentor falls.

## Case study 6.1   Fate of the caboose

Dr. Kedar Pandey had always been a larger-than-life person for as long as anybody in the organization could remember. As the Managing Director, he had taken the organization from being a reasonably well-known one in the country to being a major player in the sector in this part of the world. No mean achievement in a matter of just four years. And people looked up to him. Many thought of him as a demi-god in this business.

He had got the Prime Minister to visit the organization. Cabinet Ministers dropping in was by now a routine affair. The number of foreign dignitaries and visitors at any given time was a matter of pride to an organization that had earlier been only a small national entity. In the last few years of Dr. Pandey's tenure, the range of products and services offered by the organization had expanded to become the widest and among the best in quality and reputation. The number of foreign collaborations had grown manifold. The organization's reputation was at its highest point.

Dr. Pandey had many young executives whom he had nurtured and even, as some would put it, hand-reared. They were his loyal army—his storm-troopers, as his detractors described them. Most of these young boys and girls were bright and smart, and had the capability to get on top of any problem and work through it quickly. Dr. Pandey's hand had transformed them from being loose cannons running helter-skelter in the organization in

CONTINUED ON THE NEXT PAGE

different departments into a slick, suave, and sophisticated group of executives that anybody could be proud of. They were people who could have been brilliant in any position with a little support and backing. Dr. Pandey provided this.

There were also a few among them in this brigade who did not naturally belong. They were not as sharp as the rest, not as intelligent, not as pushy and aggressive. But they were hard workers. They would persist with the thorniest of problems, chipping away at them till they had been mastered and a solution found. These were people who could have fallen by the wayside in an aggressive and fast-paced organizational environment. Dr. Pandey protected them and they grew well in his shadow. Shahid Ahmed Ansari was one of these few.

Shahid's dependence on Dr. Pandey was absolute. People said derisively behind his back that he had sold his soul to Dr. Pandey. Shahid did not care what they said. He had enjoyed working with Dr. Pandey and had found a good and safe working environment that had recognized his capabilities and rewarded him for what he had done. The other people in the organization did not think so. They often were quick to point out that without the protective hand of Dr. Kedar Pandey, Shahid would have drowned in the competitive environment and would never in his wildest dreams have come to occupy the position he now held.

Shahid's qualifications and prior work experience had not been directly related to his present area of specialization. He had worked hard to develop himself in this area and Dr. Pandey's support in projects and assignments had helped him learn quickly. He had garnered rich experience in the field over the years he had been with Dr. Pandey. But the lack of a higher degree in the area had always been the sore point with Shahid.

CONTINUED ON THE NEXT PAGE

CASE STUDY 6.1—CONTINUED

Shahid Ansari was not a man without gratitude. He was open in his acknowledgment that he had benefited from Dr. Pandey's largesse. He had remained loyal and faithful to Dr. Pandey. He had always done Dr. Pandey's bidding, even against his better judgment. Now the judgment day, so to say, had come!

Dr. Pandey's last days in the organization were not pleasant ones. He had fallen out with the Board of Directors. They had serious difference of opinion about the direction the organization should take in the future, and to make matters worse, the Chairman had developed a personal dislike for Dr. Pandey. The final showdown resulted in the board asking Dr. Pandey to step down and for someone else to take over as a stand-in Chief Executive.

Dr. Kedar Pandey was not a man easily vanquished. He had a grand plan of leaving in a flourish, and taking with him what he considered the cream of the organization to set up one of his own. Quite a few were taken in by the eminence of the person and the grand vision his plan presented to them. In a few years they would have grown so large themselves and that too without what they considered the excess baggage of the rest of the present organization. But then, they were people who could have done well by themselves no matter where they where. Quite a few had built a support system for themselves, hedging against possible failure. But what about Shahid Ahmed Ansari?

The fall of Dr. Pandey had all those associated with him in the organization scurrying for cover. Quite a few had disowned their association with Dr. Pandey, trying to cleanse themselves of what was now considered a stain and a liability. Those that could did so, and those that couldn't had to leave.

CONTINUED ON THE NEXT PAGE

CASE STUDY 6.1—CONTINUED

This did not leave Shahid Ansari with much choice within the organization. Those of his friends who had worked closely with Dr. Kedar Pandey had chosen to leave with Dr. Pandey. But Shahid was in a dilemma. He had no security net to fall back on. Not being as affluent as the others in the group, his dependence on the organization was higher. He also had to take into consideration the responsibilities he had piled up on the family front.

Shahid's predicament of having hitched his wagon to Dr. Pandey had been compounded by the pressure of Dr. Pandey's call to Shahid to leave with him and join the nascent organization floated by Dr. Pandey. Shahid was not sure of the stability or the future of the new organization and his own future hung in the balance.

What could Shahid Ahmed Ansari do now?

## WHEN THE MENTOR FALLS

For all the virtues and the good things written about the mentor, lest we forget, the mentor is human too. There is a likelihood, however small, that the mentor may fall too.

There are good and magnanimous things to do under such circumstances. As quickly as possible, and as gracefully as possible, the mentees must be cut free so as to give them the option and choice on what to do. More than that, it is the selflessness of not wanting to drag the mentee under with you. That the mentee may wade in to aid is a choice left to the mentee, and will depend on the strength of the relationship.

However small the chances of its occurrence, it is a good idea to walk through the moves with the mentee, as one would do in a fire drill. It is better to be prepared than scurry about during a crisis.

## REACHING ACROSS THE GENERATION GAP

The mentor and the mentee are likely to be from different generations. In such a situation, there are definitely issues that need to be addressed by the mentor, and the mentee, on how their thinking, priorities and outlook can be reconciled to bring together a fruitful relationship. The responsibility devolves more on to the mentor, since she/he has the experience of encountering a wide array of issues and concerns of people.

The mentor must take on herself/himself the accountability to empathize and think like a person the of the mentee's age when dealing with the mentee. The mentee's generation has outlooks that would be fairly different from that of the mentor. There is a need to understand their priorities and how they view the world. Correct or otherwise, they do have a right to their priorities. It is the task of the mentor to have the mentee work out the efficacy of the outlook and priorities.

The younger generation has a different view of various aspects of life and has different needs. Their worldview on aspects like leisure; the need to have time to do nothing; the need not to succeed all the time; the need not to be altruistic; the need not to have an ambition for now; the need to 'chill out' and be 'cool'; the need for self-discovery before worrying about the world; perception of authority; relationship with parents, etc., may be different from that of the mentor. The mentor must have the flexibility to appreciate this in reaching across generations to connect and build a relationship.

## REVERSE MENTORING

As much as you would like to believe that you are better than some who have gone before you in any area of the profession, there are certainly people coming up behind you who may be better than you. Knowing that there are in all probability people who are better than you in some things, and being willing to learn from them, whatever their status or station in life, is a great quality to have. This openness is all the more important when you are a mentor.

There has been so much progress and so many developments in the immediate past that it is necessary to be cued in to the changes, and be able to comprehend and learn them quickly. The young are so much better at this. Therefore, there is a good chance that in a few areas the mentee is so much more proficient and capable. Here there is something for the mentor to acquire from the mentee.

There is also a good possibility that the mentee has other qualities that can be learnt by the mentor if she/he is open to doing that. A mentor who is on the journey of learning should have the humility to learn from the mentee as well.

There is so much energy and enthusiasm, so much verve and zest, so much curiosity to experiment and discover: a mentor can imbibe all these qualities from the mentee. All it takes is the openness to learn and not let anything else come in the way.

## TRANSFERENCE OF AMBITION

Ambition is individual and subjective. Each person is entitled to have her/his own ambition and also to not have one. This is something that the mentor must realize early. In doing so, the mentor will be able to appreciate the position of the mentee and help work out the best course that can take the mentee to where she/he wants. The mentor can also help the mentee understand the significance of the ambitions that she/he has, and whether the ambition is adequate or needs resetting.

There are chances that the mentor may inadvertently get the mentee to incorporate her/his own ambitions and try realize her/his ambitions through the mentee. This cannot be further away from being fair to the mentee. The mentee must be encouraged to look at and evolve her/his own ambitions without being unduly influenced by the mentor's ambitions. The mentor's intervention should only be to the extent of helping to identify and crystallize the mentee's ambitions.

## A CODE OF ETHICS FOR MENTORS

There are issues of ethics involved in the practice of mentoring. There are particular boundaries and limits to be maintained in what can or cannot be done. This is not intended to restrict and bind the freedom in a relationship of this kind, but is given as a code designed to protect those involved from getting carried away.

- The mentee's developmental needs and growth are the primary focus of the mentoring process, and the mentor's role is to address these.

- The relationship between the mentor and the mentee is mutual and all decisions and actions will be taken by mutual consent.
- The mentor and the mentee must work within the agreed terms of confidentiality and within the context of the relationship.
- Any decision to involve or refer to an external person must be taken following a discussion and mutual consent.
- The mentor and the mentee must strive to be open and truthful with each, other not only in the context of the relationship but also in the relationship itself.
- No exploitative expectations should be overtly or implicitly carried into the relationship, either by the mentor or the mentee.
- The mentor and the mentee must strive to guard the relationship and its context against misinterpretation from within and outside.
- The mentor must not intrude into the areas that the mentee does not wish to share in the relationship. Any enquiry into these areas must be with appropriate justification for it being connected to the issues involved. The mentee must respect this reciprocally too.
- The mentor must recognize and respect the individuality of the mentee and must encourage the autonomy of the mentee.
- The mentor must recognize the limits of her/his own competency and capacity and operate within them.
- The mentor must accept the responsibility and work on developing her/his own competencies and capabilities in the practice of mentoring.

- The mentor and the mentee must respect each other's time, other commitments and responsibilities to other relationships. They must be careful not to impose on each other unduly.
- The mentee must work towards accepting increasing responsibility in managing and working with the relationship as the process progresses.
- The mentor and the mentee have a mutual responsibility to discuss any move towards the dissolution of the relationship and the mentoring association with each other.
- The mentor and the mentee share equal responsibility in the smooth and graceful denouement of the process when the set purpose has been achieved.
- The mentor and mentee have an equal responsibility in avoiding the creation of dependencies.
- The mentee should be aware of her/his rights and the mentor must help the mentee understand them.
- The mentor must work within the realms of any rule or law that may be in force.

## OVERTAKING THE MENTOR

The mentor is likely to be someone who has achieved much in life already, and is quite secure in that achievement and the path ahead. But then, the mentor's achievements are no limit for what the mentee can achieve. It can well be that the mentee achieves more than the mentor, and at times also overtakes the mentor.

In these situations, the thing to bear in mind is that the mentor is never in competition with the mentee. As a great coach, the mentor should revel in the achievements of the mentee and feel proud of the fact that the mentee has out-done the mentor. This is easily said, but to really believe in it and work towards it is the essence of being a great mentor.

| Case study 6.2 | Walking ahead of the mentor |
|---|---|

The room is tastefully decorated. The desk at one end would be large enough for two, but the plush chair at its head has a regal appearance which makes sharing the space out of question. The bank of comfortable sofas at the other end of the room gives it a feeling of informality. The carpet is deep and its color matches everything else in the room—the rich wooden paneling, the upholstery and the furnishing. It is a room decorated with much care and expense.

But the man occupying the room has an appearance not wholly in keeping with the décor. He is very simply dressed in a cotton half-sleeved shirt a size too large and baggy cotton trousers. He is not very tall and his wiry frame makes him look unkempt in the loose-fitting clothes. The wispy gray mane is brushed back and appears overdue for a visit to the hairdresser. But ... he has an air about him that makes all these a matter of inconsequential detail.

He has the look of an old professor; after all, for the past several years this is what he has been. For a retired pro-fessor, he seems and feels out of place in the overdone room that is now his. However he has the humility not to make that an issue with the people who wanted him there. But what is Professor Parthasarathy doing in a set-up like this?

The room is in the Central Office of the Venkat Krishna (VK) Group of Institutions. The VK Group is owned and managed by Dr. P.V. Krishna Rao, and runs several edu-cational institutions in the city and the neighboring small towns. While quite a few of them are run on charitable lines, the rest are commercial. The VK Group has built up a very good name and reputation for itself.

CONTINUED ON THE NEXT PAGE

CASE STUDY 6.2—CONTINUED

The VK Group is the brainchild of Dr. Rao. He was a lecturer in business management in the University College more than two and a half decades ago. He had met Professor Parthasarathy then and everything had changed since then. Professor Parthasarathy was Dr. Rao's guide during the five years it took him to complete his Ph.D.

Dr. Rao too would have retired as a professor 20 years later. But not content with that, he had left his position in the university to set up a small tutorial college. Over the next 15 incredible years, he had built up a string of excellent educational institutions that could take a child from kindergarten to postgraduation. Today, Dr. Rao is among the most reputed figures in education.

That Professor Parthasarathy has been his mentor is a declaration that Dr. Rao makes frequently, and he attributes much of his success to the advice, guidance, and inspiration from Professor Parthasarathy. Dr. Rao had persuaded Professor Parthasarathy to spend his time after retirement with the VK Group. Professor Parthasarathy had declined any remuneration or position. His only task is to interact with the students and teachers of the institutions, encourage them in their academic endeavors, and, as Dr. Rao says, 'Just be there for them, as you have been there for me.' Professor Parthasarathy, living alone in an apartment across the city, now has all the time to do what he likes doing most: helping young people grow.

Dr. Rao has grown a lot since the days he had been a lecturer. He is today an advisor to the government on educational and social issues. He too has an office in the VK Group central office, next to Professor Parthasarathy's. But he has kept it smaller. Dr. Rao has, in fact, grown and has walked so much ahead of Professor Parthasarathy. But neither Professor Parthasarathy nor Dr. Rao has a problem with that.

## DEALING WITH THE MENTEE'S FAMILY

The mentee's family is a part of her/his life, and they come as a package, so to speak. As a mentor, the need to work with and carry the mentee's family along is always there, especially in the Indian social and cultural environment. Not that the mentor has any responsibility for what happens in the family, but it has to be taken into consideration to the extent that it influences the mentee's professional life. It is vital to remember that the focus should always be on the mentee.

In working with the mentee, it is good to keep the mentee's family in the loop. Helping the mentee deal with issues relating to the family should be done with discretion and caution. Also, in helping the mentee make decisions relating to personal life and the family, care must be taken to not cross mutually understood and accepted boundaries. In Indian culture and environment, the family would hold the mentor in high esteem. It is important to live up to the respect and the image. Any misunderstanding can be quite terrible for the mentoring process.

The family would have a definite role and value in the life of the mentee and she/he in theirs. The mentor has no right to usurp, in any form, the role and position of the family in the mentee's life. Even if the mentee so desires, this is still a danger area and should be treated with extreme caution. Ideally, stay out when the alarms go off.

## MENTEE'S PERSONAL RELATIONSHIPS

As a mentor, the responsibility is to look at the holistic development of the mentee. In this the personal areas of her/his life also come into view. But the mentor must respect the personal space of the mentee and not intrude. The areas of comfort and discomfort can be worked out during the exploration and while arriving at the protocol.

Even as a mentor, there is no right to information where the personal life and space are concerned. However, if events and happenings in that area are impinging into aspects of professional life, then the mentor may seek to broach the subject. The approach is to not demand information, but not to demur either in the matter. It is important to help guard against any adverse influences of personal life on the professional aspects.

In this area, it is good to remember that the role of an advisor would be better and more acceptable than that of a guardian, which the mentor clearly is not. At all times, keeping communication and dialog open would help a lot in working things out.

## MENTEE'S HEALTH

The mentee's health is the mentor's concern, and then again it is not. The line would dissolve in a haze of gray. Being that close to the mentee, the mentor should be concerned about her/his health. But it is good to remember that the mentor is not a parent.

Health is often seen as a personal issue, and unless expressly stated, is out of bounds for any intrusion from people not directly concerned. This makes the protocol and the understanding between the mentor and the mentee important in working out how far the mentor can go in looking into the state of the mentee's health.

The mentor should take any opportunity to advise the mentee on issues of health when it is beneficial to other aspects of the mentee's life. The mentor may choose to help where she/he can, and when the mentee asks for it.

## THE 'SAHIR LUDHIANVI PRINCIPLE'

One key issue is to accept that as a mentor not all efforts that are ventured into will lead to some form of success. There arise some instances in any mentor's life and work where she/he must accept that it is not working out. When things do not work out, the matter is best accepted as such.

I call it applying the 'Sahir Ludhianvi Principle.' This is after the renowned poet and lyricist of Hindi cinema, Abdul Hayie, who wrote under the *takhallus* (pen name) of Sahir Ludhianvi. Ludhianvi's lyrics have always had an opulence of inner meaning and a play of words that lingers long after the song has ended and the music has stopped playing. The profundity of some of his words reveal some deep hidden meanings in people's lives in ways that only poets can do.

In the film *Gumrah* there was a song had become quite popular: '*Chalo ek baar phir se, ajnabee ban jayen hum dono.*' The song came to be known by the first stanza, but what is important for us is a couplet that lies snuggled within. It goes:

*Woh afsana jise anjaam tak lana na ho mumkin*
*Use ke khoobsurat mod de kar chhodna achcha.*

It is tough to translate this into English with the same feel and connotation, but it translates approximately to:

That desire (dream, apparition) which it is not possible
to bring to fruition (realization, success)

> It is best to give it an interesting (lovely, beautiful) twist
> and let it go....

Only Sahir Ludhianvi could have put it in this fashion ... so much said in so few words and so lyrically rich. These words have much for the mentor to understand and imbibe.

It would certainly be good for the mentor to accept that she/he cannot be successful every time. There are times when it is more prudent to call it quits. This is when the mentor may need to discuss with the mentee that in her/his opinion things between them are not working in the manner that they should, and that it would be better if they looked at a termination of the relationship. Please remember that any decision on the relationship is ideally taken mutually.

There can be any number of reasons why things between the mentor and the mentee did not work out well, and they had to move towards an amicable end. But it is important to recognize that the relationship is terminally ill and it has moved into being dysfunctional for both (or either).

The serious caution here is that the 'Sahir Ludhianvi Principle' is not to be applied at the first sight of discord or discontent. This is a principle to be used sparingly and with extreme caution and prudence. Please do take note that the 'Sahir Ludhianvi Principle' is the very last resort, when every other effort has come to naught.

# EXPECTATIONS
# IN MENTORING

OVER the past several years, numerous workshops on mentoring and for mentors have given valuable insights into what practicing managers at various levels in different organizations expect from the mentoring process and the other players involved in the process. One important aspect of any learning is to get clarity on what is expected from the learning process itself.

The compilation given here of what the practicing and potential mentors expect from the mentee is fairly revealing.

The expectations that appeared to be more frequently expressed appear first in the list, although this is not an attempt to apply any strict ranking to the order. The italicization and the bold type are used to highlight certain issues about these expectations.

During the workshops, the mentors come up with the list of expectations after extensive discussions and sharing their experiences of the process in small groups. The expectations appear to reflect the nature of mentees who would suit the mentoring process as the mentors see it.

The italicized attributes in the list are those that attract more detailed discussion, along with the realization that they cannot be unilaterally instilled in the mentee nor be expected to come pre-packaged with the mentee. These expectations are to be worked towards mutually and built by both the mentor and the mentee working together.

The attributes given in italics are those that often get withdrawn after the discussion as being either unfair to expect or not being legitimate.

## THE MENTOR'S EXPECTATIONS OF THE MENTEE

1. Willing to take on a mentor
2. Trust
3. Confidentiality
4. Honesty
5. Openness
6. Positive attitude
7. Discipline
8. *Respect*
9. Faith in mentor and willingness to be mentored
10. *No undue favors*
11. *No financial gains*
12. Communicative
13. Flexible
14. Receptiveness
15. *Commitment and dedication*
16. Being a good listener
17. Faith
18. Sharing attitude
19. *No godfather*
20. Proactive
21. *Trustworthy*
22. *Ambitious*
23. Willing
24. Belief in the system
25. Not prone to misuse

26. Sincerity and hard work
27. Pride in the organization

The practicing managers come to realize as they carry the discussion forward that *trust* cannot actually be expected to be given by either. They had often listed this in the mistaken belief that the mentees who may come into an organization-sponsored mentoring scheme will be 'briefed' to trust their allotted or chosen mentor and be trusted by the mentor.

The same appears to go with the expectation of *trustworthiness*, and *commitment and dedication*. Both these are again the attributes and expectations that have to be built along with the strength of the relationship that comes into being between the mentor and her/his mentee. *Respect* has to be earned, whether it is by the mentor or the mentee. It cannot be expected to endure if it is taken as a prescribed and expected arrangement.

There is another group of expectations: *no godfather, no undue favors* and *no financial gains*. These are often discussed in the early stages of the workshop when the definition and the limits of the mentoring relationships are clarified. It appears that the mentors often take it for granted that the mentees will also be experiencing such an input about the process of mentoring and will understand it the same way. However, it must be realized that no matter how many times it may have been experienced by the mentee in other circumstances, it is important to articulate and state in no uncertain terms what the expected protocol in the current mentoring relationship is. This can head off misunderstandings further down the road.

*Ambitious* mentees are, on the face of it, good to have. It is akin to having been dealt a great hand in a game of cards: a matter of serendipity and good fortune. But then it is the work of the mentor to build the ambition to achieve in the mind of the mentee, who is capable of achieving greater things than she/he projects for herself/himself. The mentors do come out in the end saying that they cannot offload their responsibility in this manner.

The mentors often tend to discuss the desirable more frequently than focusing on what need to be done if a mentee comes in without these attributes. These are expectations of what attributes the mentors would like their mentees to have; but if the mentee is packaged so perfectly, the mentors may find themselves on the redundancy list! This is a common refrain.

## THE MENTEE'S EXPECTATIONS FROM THE MENTOR

1. Time
2. Accessible
3. Good communicator
4. Sensitive
5. Empathy and understanding
6. Protector
7. Good listener
8. Professional competency
9. Influential person
10. Godfather
11. Career planning
12. Genuine interest in holistic growth
13. Knowledge and professional guidance
14. Trust and confidentiality
15. Objectivity

16. Love and affection
17. Caring and sharing
18. Having choice of mentor
19. Pleasant and friendly
20. Patience
21. Appreciation
22. Human relations skills
23. Well-wisher
24. Motivator
25. Cooperative
26. Friend
27. Coach
28. Honest and a role model
29. Trust
30. Emotional support
31. Human touch
32. Participate in mentee's endeavors
33. Skilled in networking
34. Understand work culture
35. Confidence

Mentees are frequently far more cautious and less expansive about what to expect from the mentor. They tend to be less clear in their mind about their expectations and sometimes express them as what they tend to be comfortable with. There is also a leaning towards a let's-wait-and-watch approach.

There are also quite a few who are quite clear about what they are looking for, and these are the mentees who are willing to go for what they want. These also tend to be aggressive in seeking mentors and do go to the extent of questioning potential mentors incisively during contact sessions arranged by the organizational schemes.

The expectation of getting a *protector*, *influential person*, or a *godfather* as a mentor is a masked desire and is slyly slipped in during discussions. The mentees do overtly aver that they are not in favor of such practices, but in unguarded moments they give in to the hope that they may get a mentor to fast-track them up the corporate ladder.

Here again, *trust* and *friendship* are frequently taken for granted and it is not realized until pointed out that this is something that has to be worked upon and earned. The expectation is perhaps that someone else will do this for them when they work within the organizational context.

The following list contains collated observations from the discussions and sessions that the mentees have gone through in the numerous workshops conducted for them in different organizations over the years. They are indicative of the thinking of young people eager to make good in their career and life with their mentor.

## BEHAVIORS IN THE MENTOR THAT THE MENTEES LIKE

1. Offers new and creative perspectives on life which do not strike the mentee
2. Down-to-earth and pragmatic
3. Openly shows faith in you
4. Open to call 24/7, always makes time
5. Organized, in control and patient
6. Can be asked about anything, any time and without ascribing any reason for asking (within limits)
7. Persuasive and amiable
8. Open to other points of view
9. Willing to listen

10. Has abundant information on a wide variety of subjects
11. Criticizes constructively and is supportive
12. Can relate to your level of understanding and experience
13. Sets a good example—a role model
14. Warm and smiling
15. Persuades you to change
16. Always working towards success
17. Shares expertise in her/his field easily
18. Experienced, but young at heart
19. Committed to the cause of mentoring
20. Good energizer and morale booster

## BEHAVIORS IN THE MENTOR THAT THE MENTEES DISLIKE

1. Authoritarian and controlling
2. Not enthusiastic about the process and the scheme
3. Tries to make time, but does not give mentoring priority
4. Does not keep to committed time
5. Lets bias overtake judgment
6. Does not consider other points of view
7. Does not keep in constant touch
8. Likes to talk more than listen
9. Talks around the problem and does not approach it
10. Vague about how she/he can help you
11. Loner; does not socialize
12. Outdated views and values
13. Not open to new ideas and unwilling to consider other points of view

14. Unsure of mentoring role
15. Lacks depth in her/his chosen field
16. Unable to inspire mentee
17. Negative and pessimistic attitude
18. Indecisive and unsure

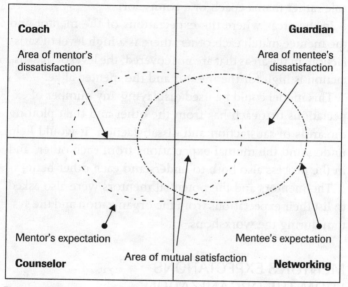

**Figure 7.1**
Mentor and mentee expectation and satisfaction

Plotting the expectations of the mentor against what she/he can offer the mentee in the process of mentoring, and also plotting the expectations of the mentee would give an interesting picture of where the mentor and the mentee find mutual satisfaction and individual dissatisfaction.

These are four attributes of the mentor that we have taken to illustrate what could happen in the process of mentoring. The mentor has expectations of what she/he should be or do for the mentee in the course of the mentoring relationship. Being a coach and a counselor may be a higher priority for the mentor, while also playing the lesser roles of being a guardian and helping in networking. At the same time, the priority of the mentee may be a little different. She/he may be expecting more of a guardianship and networking role rather than a coach or a counselor.

In the areas where the expectations of the mentor and the mentee match each other, there is a high level of satisfaction. In the areas that are not covered, the level of dissatisfaction is high for the mentor and the mentee alike.

This model could be used displaying any number of expectations that each has from the other and then plotting the areas of satisfaction and dissatisfaction. It would help understand the mutual expectations from each other, and in the process also both to understand each other better.

The mentors and the potential mentors were also asked to list their expectations from the organization and the system during the workshops.

## MENTOR'S EXPECTATIONS FROM THE ORGANIZATION

1. Adequate training
2. Self-development resources
3. Choice of mentor/mentee
4. No intervention (intrusion)
5. Relationship should be respected within organization
6. *Recognition*
7. Refresher for mentors
8. Literature and feedback on practices in other organizations

9. Not to be a part of the evaluation process
10. Develop culture of mentoring
11. Should not be part of KRA (Key Result Area)
12. Access to policies
13. *Time for mentoring*
14. *Keep mentor informed about decisions affecting mentee*
15. *Infrastructure for mentors*
16. Mentor–mentee meets
17. Involvement to promote system
18. Celebration
19. Mentors' club
20. Feedback on the mentoring process
21. Moral and ethical support
22. Freedom to deal with the mentee

Recognition, time for mentoring, and infrastructure are often quietly withdrawn when the realization dawns on the mentors during the discussions that this hands the control of the process to the system, and there is a good likelihood of monitoring and evaluation of the process stepping in. It is good to be as little dependent on organizational prop-up to keep the process going as possible. The organizations may in their own interest, though, choose to provide these supports to build and nurture the mentoring efforts. Further, officially asking for information on the mentee may tread on the line manager's toes at times. The mentors agree that it is better to let the mentee inform them.

There is also a list created by the mentors after the discussions on what they think the organizations expect from them.

## ORGANIZATION'S EXPECTATIONS FROM MENTORS

1. Self-development effort
2. Organizational culture and growth
3. Retention
4. Core value actualization
5. Confidence building among both
6. Knowledge and value transfer
7. Eventually, higher productivity and better HRM
8. Learning organization
9. Lower stress levels
10. Mentors remaining in organization
11. Responsible human beings
12. Voluntarily keeping this movement alive
13. Competent group of professionals
14. Continuation of mentoring chain
15. No degeneration of the mentoring system
16. Produce winners
17. Homogeneity of culture
18. Commitment and dedication
19. Value-based workforce
20. Feeling of belonging to organization

| Case study 7.1 | Iqbal |
| --- | --- |

Iqbal S. has come up the hard way. He is the fourth of six children: two boys and four girls. His mother held a clerical job in the Indian Railways, given on compassionate grounds after his father died in service when Iqbal was very young.

CONTINUED ON THE NEXT PAGE

CASE STUDY 7.1—IQBAL (CONTD.)

His older brother is also employed in the Railways, but lives on his own after his marriage failed due to his alcoholism. His mother supports two of his sisters, one separated and the other as yet unmarried.

Iqbal had to struggle to complete his engineering course, yet did well enough to top the college. He completed his MBA from one of the national institutes on a scholarship. He has worked with two other organizations in about three years before he came to work in Indus Industries Ltd., as Assistant Manager.

Iqbal is 28 years old. He explains away two years that he has lost in his career due to bad company and habits as part of his struggle in coping with a poor and lower-middle-class background. He claims to have made the movement towards sincerity and good character.

Iqbal's immediate supervisor is a little wary of him. He finds Iqbal very useful and effective at work. But he is not very sure of how far Iqbal can be relied upon. Iqbal has so far been efficient and has completed the tasks assigned to him with diligence and care. He is meticulous and sharp. However he has had a problem with sticking to time schedules.

He has met you a couple of times and has spoken well to you. A couple of days ago he spoke to you about seeking your 'advice' on whether he should continue in the company, and on how he should work his career to escape his difficult past.

Would you take Iqbal as a mentee? What would be your approach to helping him?

CONTINUED ON P. 169

## Case study 7.2    Ash

Ashwini Kumar likes to be called Ash. Friends use this in preference to the full name and this pleases Ash very much. Ash is quick to show happiness and is very considerate to friends. There is no dearth of people who consider Ash their good friend.

Being popular, Ash leads a busy life. Work at the office never seems to finish. No sooner does office work for the day come to a close, the whirl of friends' starts. Ash is liked by most of the bosses at work, but there has been talk recently about some unfinished work and tardy progress on some important projects. But most people have found it difficult to complain about Ash lest they get isolated in the act.

Ash had grown up in Mumbai's well-to-do suburbs and had always been a happy child. Both parents are medical doctors and are well known in their fields. They have been leading busy lives, as super-specialists do. Ash is their only child. Ambition has never been a part of Ash's thinking. Yet the results throughout the undergraduate years and postgraduate study in economics have always been well above average.

Ash has joined the Corporate Planning Cell of Indus Industries Ltd. as an Assistant Manager. Being selected with good references, there have been high expectations from Ash.

Ash has confessed to you about being confused as to where all this headed. Ash is not even sure about making a choice between a career and a soft life. 'Friends, yes; work, yes; fun, yes; achievements, yes; praise, yes; life, yes; but where is it all taking me?'

Would you take Ash as a mentee? What would be your approach to helping Ash?

CONTINUED ON THE NEXT PAGE

## Case study 7.1 | Iqbal (continued)

There is no quick-fix, one-step solution for Iqbal. The thing to be noticed in Iqbal's case is that in no aspect of his life has he had any form of stability. In his personal life, social life, and professional life, he has been in constant search of an anchor.

Enabling him to find this would be a good idea. Finding his feet in his professional life and sticking to one job for a period of time without restlessness and trouble is the eventual objective. It is, however, important to also work with his family in trying to get him a stable environment, as his 'friends' have not been reliable in the past.

Counseling him to help curb and manage his restless energy at the workplace, while also encouraging him to work with his family to settle down now that he is 28, is a good approach.

## Case study 7.2 | Ash (continued)

Ashwini Kumar has had the luxury of having everything in life. A comfortable early life, good education, a good job.... Now the problem is to decide on what to do next.

Now, nowhere in the preceding part of the case does it say that Ash is a boy.... So, what would be your approach if Ash is a girl?

The situation changes altogether if the mentor needs to think about the options for a girl or for a boy in the Indian environment. As everywhere else, the boy needs to work and hold down a job, even if it is as an entrepreneur. But in the Indian environment, there is a likelihood of a different outlook for a girl. Except for economic reasons, which do not apply to Ash, the girl need not look at a job as a necessity.

CONTINUED ON THE NEXT PAGE

CASE STUDY 7.2—ASH (CONTD.)

If Ash is taken to be a boy, then he needs help in identifying his strengths and setting his priorities, to get working at finding focus on the job and getting his act together.
Separating his social life from his professional life is going
to be a priority.

If Ash is taken to be a girl then the options are different.
Here she needs help in identifying what she wants to do
with herself in the first place. Does holding a job fit in with
the scheme of things she has for herself? If not, then what
would she like to do? And having got these issues clarified,
what would be the best avenue for her to find herself comfortable and happy again?

# MENTORING SCHEMES IN ORGANIZATIONS

THERE are several advantages to be had from encouraging mentoring within the organization. Whether by design or coming up as uncontrolled mushrooming growth, mentoring provides not only the young and the lower echelons of the organization an opportunity to move forward, but also helps those at the higher and 'safer' branches of the organization tree an opportunity to participate in the organization's future.

## WHY ORGANIZATIONS ENCOURAGE MENTORING

Let us take a look at why organizations would want to invest in this direction:

1. Leveraging organizational knowledge and experience pool
2. Better-trained staff
3. Stronger bonds and network
4. Unified organizational culture
5. Effective management development
6. Stronger learning orientation
7. Non-intrusive learning
8. Greater satisfaction

9. Stronger identification with organization
10. Possibility of reduced employee turnover

Over time the organization builds a substantial pool of experience and knowledge vested in its people. This pool stays with the people and leaves with them, unless the organization is able to design systems to use or retain the valuable resource for its own use. In mentoring, the organization has an excellent device to leverage this resource, and the direct result would be people with better capabilities and knowledge.

This is also a great opportunity for creating a unified and homogeneous organizational culture, oriented towards continuous learning and development. Mentoring, as a people development tool, is non-intrusive in nature and is thus a far more acceptable method aimed at substantial utility of learning in the long term.

A direct benefit is the affable manner in which the absorption of the coming generation of people into the organizational culture takes place in mentoring and the building of stronger identity with the organization. This may slowly lead into increased retention of staff, i.e., a decline in people turnover.

## THE DOWNSIDE OF MENTORING IN ORGANIZATIONS

Like all initiatives and efforts at management development and management practices, the mentoring intervention is not without its downside and risks. However, the advantages, if harnessed and worked through with care and commitment, do substantially outweigh the downside. Some of the downsides are:

1. Raising employee expectations
2. Failure of mentoring scheme for any reason could vitiate organizational culture and relationships
3. Organization could become insular and incestuous in development and growth
4. Raising levels of insecurity and conflict if the scheme is not communicated well
5. Could add to work and work pressure in an already high-pressure work environment if adequate care is not taken

## ORGANIZATION-SPONSORED VS. INDIVIDUAL MENTORING IN ORGANIZATIONS

The question that then arises is whether the mentoring scheme should be corporate-sponsored or the organization should merely facilitate individual mentoring initiatives to take root and bloom. There is much to be said on either side. The choice is to be made after weighing all the factors and issues.

### Advantages of organization-sponsored mentoring

1. There is a specific ownership of the initiative
2. Designated and committed team or individual helping in directing or providing direction to the overall scheme

3. The whole scheme is planned and structured
4. The mentor and potential mentors are likely to be selected on criteria advantageous to the process, scheme, and organization
5. The mentors and potential mentors are likely to be briefed and/or trained in the process
6. Mentors are likely to have greater clarity and a clearer view of the organizational objectives and individual benefits
7. The mentors are likely to be well cued-in to the organizational network and functioning
8. There is likely to be parity among mentors for similar groups of mentees
9. The mentors are likely to be a good organizational resource
10. There is less likelihood of conflict with the line managers during the process
11. Top management and organizational support is easier obtained
12. There is greater uniformity in practice across the organization

## Disadvantages of organization-sponsored mentoring

1. Unified scheme may restrict freedom
2. Role and responsibility conflicts may arise for mentors with line relationships with mentees
3. Mentors may take the scheme as a part of the job and the personal commitment may fall short
4. Organizational interest may override individual requirements

5. Farmed approach may counteract attempts at customization of practices and relationships
6. Choice of mentors may not be left wholly to mentees or vice versa
7. Shortfall in system or owner commitment may derail the entire process

Individual mentors working at creating their own little enterprise could also be another approach that could accrue benefits to the individual and the organization. Organizational culture being supportive, the organization could provide the sub-stratum for such a mushrooming crop. Here too, there is the bright side and the gray side.

## Advantages of individual mentoring in organizations

1. Mentor–mentee relationship is more spontaneous and less constrained
2. Mentors likely to be of high standing in their individual field
3. Mentoring not constrained by the organizational perception of norms, suggestions or impositions (greater freedom to explore)
4. Relation is often the focal point and mentoring is less likely to be task focused
5. Individual benefits and growth override corporate requirements
6. Relationship not pressured into meeting any success criterion
7. Mentee less likely to suspect the mentor's motives
8. Mentor more likely to be driven by altruistic values

## Disadvantages of individual mentoring in organizations

1. No element of protection for mentees; no guarantees
2. No control over quality of mentors
3. Mentor may not be trained
4. Mentor may not meet organizational expectations
5. Mentors themselves may not have adequate control over the process
6. No facilitation or support available for the relationship
7. No recognition of success
8. No safety net for failures
9. May be less work-related

# INTERNAL VS. EXTERNAL MENTORS

The choice, then, is also about whether an internal mentor would be more functional than an external one. Home-grown mentors may have their own worth in the organizational scheme of things, but the virtue of having an external mentor is not to be forgotten.

## Internal mentor

1. Understands the organization and its needs intimately and from the inside
2. Would also be cued-in to the internal dynamics of the organization
3. Would have a better measure of the interpersonal dynamics between people and the relationships within the organization

4. Would have greater stakes in the organization
5. Would be clearer about the organizational issues relating to growth and career progression
6. May bring in excessive subjectivity to the process
7. Being intimately a part of the processes in the organization, may not be able to rise above them
8. May have perspectives and views constrained by the bounds of the organization
9. May become more work- and task-focused than required
10. May make the whole process incestuous

## External mentor

1. Is not connected with the internal dynamics, so can take an independent perspective
2. Relationship and individual development take precedence
3. Is not bound by the requirements of the organization —can make unbound choices and decisions
4. Brings in newer and fresher perspectives
5. Does not have an axe to grind, so may not come in with a fixed solution
6. Has the liberty to question set routines and 'sacred' rituals in the organization
7. Does not have to pay obeisance to organizational authority
8. May not be fully aware of organizational dynamics, so may miss subtleties
9. May lack organizational support to the process

# ORGANIZATIONAL CULTURE AND PREPAREDNESS FOR THE MENTORING SCHEME

Does the organization have a culture that supports and fosters mentoring schemes? Like a delicate sapling, a nascent mentoring scheme needs good support from the soil, the sub-stratum, and the caretaker. Wrong weather, climate or soil would mean a quick end to the sapling's life. Mentoring schemes tend to wither away quickly if not nurtured by the right organizational climate and culture and by the sponsors of the scheme.

A few questions to be asked before taking the call on whether the organization and its culture are ready for the introduction of the mentoring scheme intervention:

- Is there a predominant faith among the people that the organizational systems are fair and equitable?
- Is there an overall feeling of mutual comfort and trust between superiors and subordinates?
- Is there functional harmony in the atmosphere in the organization?
- Are communication channels free and open in the organization?
- Do people sense an overall feeling of satisfaction in growth and career development?
- Does the organization foster learning and self-development?
- Is commitment and loyalty to the organization pre-dominant in the organization?
- Are unhealthy rivalries and conflicts discouraged and put down?

Most, if not all, these conditions being a part of the organizational practices and life enable a good culture and environment to nurture and help a mentoring scheme take root in the organization. In such situations people tend to be positively oriented and give nascent developmental schemes a fair equitable opportunity to justify themselves and flourish.

Beyond the environment and culture is the issue of system and resource support that is formally available in the organization. There also has to be a tangible faith within the organization and the decision-making set-up regarding the efficiency of development schemes such as these.

Among the crucial requirements is that 'management' —at whatever level and connotation applicable in the organization—should view HRD as a priority and a definite real-value investment. Falling short in this could stifle the scheme at birth itself, or at a later date during its lifetime. Organizational readiness to work towards the introduction of a mentoring scheme hinges heavily on this factor.

Availability of adequate financial support is good for the health of the mentoring scheme. In any case there isn't much by way of financial outlay that is called for, but a management that is already tight-fisted about expenditure on HRD may look askance at even the smallest outflow. This could lead to skepticism and disillusionment among those in the scheme.

Just as crucial is the credibility of the HRD team with the rest of the organization. An HRD team that has a high level of acceptance and credibility finds that the ideas and schemes they initiate do well even in turbulent, and at times unfavorable, times and climates. A mentoring scheme would definitely have better chances of success in an organization that has a good and credible HRD team.

A vital aspect of the readiness of the organization is the attitude of the managers themselves towards learning and development and HRD. Having the managers believe in the virtues of a good learning and development scheme would go a long way towards sustaining the scheme itself. The managers in the organization should see value in investment in this direction.

Further, it will augur well if the managers allow time and opportunity for the employees to engage in training and development activities, and accord these activities priority over other tasks which are non-critical. Another related issue is the extent to which the employees themselves seek and utilize development opportunities.

An organization that recognizes good work towards growth and development of others; that fosters innovation and risk-taking; and that rewards accomplishments in learning and development would be well on the path to being an ideal one for the mentoring scheme to succeed in. These are good indications of an organization with a high level of preparedness.

There are finally a few small but important steps left in checking the preparedness of the organization. Will there be an adequate number of senior people in the organization willing to take on the role of mentors? Will they persist to the very end with the relationship and the commitment? It is always prudent to get a good idea about this before venturing any further.

One small, but equally significant, thing is to check if there are any learning and development schemes (like coaching, secondment, etc.) that might conflict with the mentoring scheme.

# SETTING UP AND IMPLEMENTING A MENTORING SCHEME

## 1. Designing the scheme

Getting an overview of the approach, the requirements and the expectations is a good first step to work forward from. If the organization has done some work earlier in needs analysis or learning and development requirements, it will add value to the scheme and its implementation.

Focus on gaining clarity about the organizational goals and the management plans for the organization. The business needs, both current and in the future, and the anticipated barriers to these could help in judging how the scheme could take shape in the coming period of time.

These inputs help in giving the scheme a concrete shape, especially if learning and development is a crucial requirement and input in the scheme of things. Part of the design approach is checking the training component of the learning and development approach. Then again, one must examine how mentoring can add substantially and significantly to the strategy.

The design should ideally visualize the structural approach to the scheme. The time frame and the sequence of steps in the intervention should be clearly charted, along with the cost estimates and the financial outlay for each step, and the expected outputs and the indicators of success.

The design document outlining the scheme should ideally contain the following:

1. The approach and purpose of mentoring as an developmental intervention in the organization

2. The specific reason why it is being introduced in the organization (the value addition to the organization; the objectives it is trying to achieve; who are the likely beneficiaries, etc.)
3. Broad objectives sought to be achieved
4. Broad outputs or results expected
5. Who (department, group, person) is sponsoring or putting up or organizing the scheme
6. A brief description of the approach or steps involved in the implementation of the scheme (in sequence)
7. People-support that will be required (potential mentors, administrators of the scheme, backing of the top management team, etc.)
8. Broad time-frame for the achievement of indicated landmarks
9. Time investment required by the people involved (implementation team, mentors, mentees, facilitators, back-office support people)
10. Financial commitment estimated during the currency of the scheme (if possible include the opportunity costs of the time of the people involved)
11. Contact details of the people directly involved in designing and sponsoring the scheme

The design is the integral part of the proposal that will be sent for approval and to seek the necessary mandate to carry it forward.

## 2. Defining expectations, parameters, and goals

Why are we seeking to establish and run this scheme in the organization? What do we expect to achieve? Who will gain from it? How many will gain? Who will help in getting it done? How many of them? What do they expect to gain from it? When will all this happen? In how many phases? What gains are there to be had? What do we expect that the top management will have to do to help? Who are the target beneficiaries? What limitations are being visualized for this scheme and the mentors involved? What are the specific landmarks or indicators planned? And, finally, how much will all this cost?

A neat bunch of questions. Getting answers to these will be a must before we can take the scheme forward. Each organization has its own unique answer to each of the questions.

The best way to get to it will be to have the implementation team brainstorm the answers. It is vital that the expectations, objectives, and goals are as specific and clear as they can get, for the phases of the scheme that will follow depend largely on this.

## 3. Constituting the core implementation team

The core implementation team should ideally comprise:

- The implementation leader/champion
- The scheme coordinator
- The training and development specialist
- The external consultant (where necessary)

Each person listed here has specific and vital roles contributing to the success of the scheme. Being careful in getting the right person to carry out the tasks and the expectations is an important caution. It really pays to be careful in this.

### The mentoring champion

- Should be committed and enthusiastic about the scheme
- Should be highly energetic and motivated
- Should be capable of motivating and providing drive
- Should be quite familiar with the mentoring process
- Should be good at managing projects and interventions
- Should be well respected in the organization
- Should have a high level of influence in the organization
- Should be on excellent terms with the top management or belong to the top management
- Should have excellent relationship and people management skills
- Should be suave and diplomatic in dealing with people
- Should be willing to invest time and effort in the mentoring scheme

It is always an excellent idea to choose a leader or champion for the scheme who has by herself/himself a high standing in the organizational scheme of things, maybe someone from the top management itself. A person with good influencing and networking skills to make things happen would be an ideal candidate for the job. But added to this must be a genuine interest in the mentoring scheme. In one sense, the scheme must ride on her/his shoulders in the initial phases and not vice versa.

### Role of the mentoring coordinator

The coordinator is the principal 'working' agent of the scheme. She/he has a role that is the backbone of the scheme. Such a person should:

- Be the clearing-house of all information and data relating to the mentoring intervention within the organization
- Be the visible and public face of the mentoring intervention within and outside the organization
- Be an advocate for the scheme
- Arrange and manage as much publicity for the scheme as possible to build awareness and interest
- Help in identifying the potential mentors
- Arrange for their training and 'ramp-up'
- Arrange for refresher training and other inputs where necessary
- Prepare information (and publicity) material to facilitate the functioning of mentors and mentees
- Ensure logistic and material support where necessary and possible
- Manage the budget and budgetary support
- Facilitate the review mechanism and ensure timely completion of the processes

The team would be at the apex level. As the implementation gets going it would be necessary to form action teams at the implementation level and geographic locations. Here it will be necessary to co-opt additional members to strengthen the support and assistance that will be required at the ground level. Action teams at the local level should have:

- Unit/project-level facilitator
- Administrative support
- Unit/project-level counselor

These roles may overlap and may be combined, depending on the capability of the people involved, their interest and the environment at the local level.

In any case the base requirement is that all those coming on board the implementation team should be clear and committed to the mentoring process and the scheme. Thorough briefing of the team is essential, not only to sustain their morale, but also to extend it to the constituents they work with.

## 4. Seeking top management support

It is always a good move to enlist a buy-in from the top management before the initiation and implementation of any learning and development scheme. It must also be kept in mind that the more involved, enthusiastic and passionate the top management is about the scheme, the greater its chances of perpetuation in the organization and its eventual success.

What is also important to remember is that the buy-in at the corporate level does not necessarily imply enthusiastic participation in implementation at the different installations and offices across the organization. What one should aim at is wide acceptance, so as to provide the nascent scheme the best start possible.

Ideally, target the individuals or groups whose backing and sponsorship, patronage and name would give the scheme the impetus at the start. Briefing them in as much detail as possible about what mentoring is, how it works, the enormous advantages and benefits to the individuals and the organization, the comparatively low costs involved, the benefits of leveraging the existing knowledge and experience base in the organization, etc., are good selling points.

Do also mention the risks involved and the areas or situations that could lead to failure. It will also be a good idea to mention here as a precaution some of the downside of mentoring. At the same time, add the cautions being taken to pre-empt and prevent their happening here.

## 5. Publicizing the scheme and gaining/ seeking wider support within the organization

When the top management has a buy-in into the scheme, the scheme is on its way. However, that alone will often be found inadequate. The scheme must get a much wider acceptance within the organization. This ensures a smoother and easier path during the running and establishment of the scheme.

Getting wider participation and also acceptance of the scheme is crucial for its longevity and effectiveness. This also helps in answering and countering skepticism that is almost always inherent in any organization when it comes to learning and development initiatives. This is true especially when there is an action expectation from the participants. Wider publicity and open communication about the scheme will work well towards wider participation in the long run.

Communiqués, open forums, presentations, newsletters, discussion groups, etc., are good methods to get the message across. Persistent and consistent communication for a long period before the scheme is formally announced will serve well in most organizations.

## 6. Identifying potential mentors and mentees

Potential mentors in the organization can be identified based on criteria that will help pick the best available talent for the mission. The thing to remember is that being a mentor is a voluntary activity and should not be imposed. The mentors should not be conscripted lest they end up looking at the scheme and activity as another part of a job they are performing.

One way of going about identifying potential mentors is to first get the criteria for 'qualifying' in place. First list those qualities that are central to the organization and the mentoring process. These brook no compromise in potential mentors. These are criteria like integrity, communication skills, experience and maturity, commitment, acceptability, learning and development orientation, etc.

Other qualities could be add-ons that contribute and help in the process. Here the qualities to look for are leadership, interpersonal skills, success orientation, focus and dedication, task focus, personal success, etc.

Be open enough to publicize the qualities being sought and the criteria for qualifying in the scheme. There is the likelihood of a certain level of competitiveness and politics involved in the 'selection' and 'volunteering' process. This has to be clearly and firmly discouraged if the future and continuance of the scheme is to be assured. It will be good to have a list of volunteers from whom the short-listing of mentors can be done. There may be variations of this approach that can be taken depending on the nature and culture of the organization. But please do bear in mind that the objective is to get the best available potential mentors into the scheme and not compromise the scheme in pursuit of getting the required numbers.

With regard to mentees it is a good idea to have an open forum for all interested to make clear the broad purpose, parameters and expectations from the scheme before calling for volunteers. This is primarily to protect the scheme from interlopers who seek to make a quick gain from the opportunity to plug into the network of senior executives who may come in as mentors. A list similar to that for mentors can be drawn up for the mentees too.

## 7. Training mentors and mentees

Before taking the potential mentors and the mentees forward in the journey of mentoring and taking the implementation of the scheme any further, making sure that they have the requisite understanding of what they are getting into is essential. The chosen people must undergo formal training to clarify their understanding of the role expectations from them, not just for the good of organization and the scheme, but also for their own benefit.

It is advisable to conduct the training or workshops for the mentors and the mentees separately. Boxes 8.1 and 8.2 give some details about training programs that could be conducted.

| Box 8.1 | One-day workshop for mentees |

The workshop has the primary objective of introducing the concept of mentoring to the potential mentees. It also serves to clarify any misgivings or false expectations that they may harbor about the process and the scheme.

Suggested broad content:

- Building a career as a professional (organizational environment, organizational structure, career path, success factors, pitfalls and bottlenecks, etc.)
- Mentoring as a facilitative intervention (background and development, advantages, benefits, past experiences, etc.)
- Guidelines for mentees and mentors (who, what, when, where, and how)
- Downside of mentoring for the mentees
- Introducing the organizational mentoring scheme (design, implementation team, information and resources available, etc.)
- Sharing mutual expectations (mentees' expectations, mentors' expectations, discussion on legitimacy of expectations, etc.)
- Explaining the mentoring process (how it proceeds, importance of the relationship, landmarks to look for, etc.)
- Evaluation and monitoring process

| Box 8.2 | Two-day workshop for mentors |

The objectives of this workshop include not only reinforcing the concepts of good mentoring, but also walking the mentors through the cautions and care they need to keep in mind in the process. The workshop also aims to take the

CONTINUED ON THE NEXT PAGE

BOX 8.2—CONTINUED

mentors through a self-inventory of the skills and competencies with regard to mentoring.

While Day 1 of the workshop is intended to get clarity on the role and the mentoring process, Day 2 is to be devoted to getting a better understanding about self, and the skills and competencies involved in mentoring.

Suggested broad content:

- Understanding the role and character of the mentor (clarity of definition, who the mentor is and is not, background and development of mentoring, etc.)
- Mentoring as a people developmental method (concept and practice, how the method fits in with the overall people development strategy, etc.)
- Introducing organizational mentoring scheme (design, approach and objectives, time frame, implementation team, information and resources available, etc.)
- Understanding expectations from the mentoring process (mentors' expectation, mentees' expectations, organizational expectations, discussion on the tenability of the expectations and the ways to meet them, etc.)
- Evaluation and monitoring components in the mentoring scheme
- Understanding the values and attitudes that facilitate mentoring
- Understanding the skills and competencies required in mentoring (self-exploration and inventory, interpretation and suggestions for consolidation and development, etc.)

These workshops can be followed by contact sessions, if these form a part of the design under the scheme. The clarity that the workshops can provide to both mentors and mentees will help them make appropriate and optimal use of the opportunity that the contact session can provide.

## 8. The contact session

The contact session is the meeting where the prospective mentors and the mentees may meet formally for the first time. There are advantages in the mentoring implementation team choosing to arrange the meeting. The principal advantage is in ensuring that the meeting goes off smoothly and that the process is afoot. There is also the advantage of having a common person—who could be anybody from the mentoring team—who can make the necessary introduction. However, there is also the disadvantage of the team having to match mentor to mentee instead of leaving the match-up to the choices of the mentors and the mentees.

On the other hand, if other systems have been evolved for the mentor and the mentee to meet informally in some other setting or location, the informality of the relationship gets a boost. In this, however, there is also the possibility of the process going out of the purview of the mentoring scheme and would make it difficult to judge the health of the process.

There is a method that can, in a sense, have the advantages of both. If the number of mentors and mentees is manageable, then a session with both the prospective mentors and the mentees can be arranged. In this session, each prospective mentor has the opportunity to meet each mentee who has subscribed to the scheme. Using a carousel method, each mentor spends a reasonable time with each mentee. At the end of the session everyone in the session has had an opportunity to interact and be introduced to everyone else. This session may be repeated if the need is felt for this.

The mentor and the mentees are given a chance to short-list the people whom they might like to meet again to seek further interaction to firm up their choice. Giving them a reasonable period of time to work this out is a good idea, after which the matter can be followed up individually. In this the mentor and the mentee do get a say in whom they are associated with in the mentoring scheme. The mentoring team will have to sort out overlaps and clarify choices where necessary.

The scheme is now well under way. It would be a good initiative to stay with the mentor and mentee pairs for a further period of time, hand-holding them till they are able to reach the stage of arriving at a mutual agreement in the mentoring context.

## 9. Providing support and back-up

The implementation team and the organization have a responsibility to provide the mentor and the mentee with support and back-up. The thing to remember is that these should not have any strings or controls attached. Having ensured the selection of people with the right set of values and attitudes into the scheme, the popular excuse of 'preventing misuse' cannot be used to retain control.

The support that might be expected is in the nature of getting more information on mentoring itself; administrative clarifications; clearing doubts about relationships; clarifications on organizational system or structure; provision of minor facilities; arranging a common forum for mentors and mentees; and, at times, the need for a counselor. Having committed to the scheme, supporting and backing it up at this stage is definitely a big help.

Beyond this the implementation team needs to just keep watch without actually intervening in the relationship and the process. Only in situations of dire necessity is stepping in warranted. Just being there is important and gives the scheme support.

## 10. Monitoring and evaluation

Like any developmental intervention, the mentoring scheme also comes in with the demand for evaluation of its effectiveness. Here is the rub: mentoring is unlike other schemes, and cannot be treated like them. Monitoring the mentoring scheme a little too closely interferes with the process and so does an attempt to evaluate the progress of the process or the quality of the relationship.

The main reasons often given for measuring the mentoring intervention include:

1. To monitor the relative efficiency of the scheme
2. To take a diagnostic check on the ongoing relationships
3. To get feedback on the working of the scheme
4. To demonstrate the worth of the investment into the scheme
5. To encourage greater participation in the scheme

Situations where measurements of the intervention are detrimental:

1. Assessment is for reporting on progress of individual to a third person or party
2. To assess the performance of the mentor, linking it to mentoring
3. Attempting to link the mentors' judgment to a reward mechanism for the mentee
4. Assessing the quality and content of the discussion between the mentor and the mentee
5. Attempt to relatively grade mentors or the performance of different mentors

A good way to understand and assess the effectiveness of the scheme is to take it informally. Talking to the mentors and the mentees in the scheme and getting them to give a subjective measure of its utility and progress would give a fairly good idea. Also, an understanding of the progress of the process can be obtained from the suggestions for change and improvements given by those involved. Pushing beyond this is like plucking the plant out to see if the roots are growing, which is not at all a good idea.

# FAQ ON MENTORING

## 1. How is mentoring different from executive coaching?

EXECUTIVE coaching is focused on imparting skills and competencies for making the person more effective in her/his job or position. Mentoring is a far more long-term association and includes most aspects of executive coaching. Mentoring is a developmental intervention for the holistic advancement of the individual, encompassing growth and gaining greater maturity in the professional, personal and social aspects too.

## 2. Is the mentor always a man or can there be women mentors?

Sure, there can be women mentors too. All that is required is that the relationships and the process of mentoring are taken care of—being a man or a woman does not contribute to or detract from effectiveness. There are however, certain gender-related concerns to be kept in mind while working with a mentor of the other sex. Cross-gender mentoring has issues of its own (see Chapter 6).

## 3. How often should the mentor and the mentee meet?

There isn't a fixed frequency that can be prescribed. The frequency of meetings depends on the stage of development of the mentoring relationship, the urgency of the issue being addressed and the requirements of the mentee. Whatever frequency both are comfortable with and meets the needs of the process is fine.

### 4. How do we evaluate the effectiveness of mentoring?

Evaluating the effectiveness of mentoring is a contentious issue. There is a delicate balance between gathering information to give an adequate measure of the success of mentoring and intruding into the sanctity of the mentor–mentee relationship. Where the line is to be drawn and does eventually get drawn in an organization-sponsored mentoring scheme is the issue that often causes much heartache. There has to be extreme caution and a lot of discretion before stepping into this area. The best would be to gather informal feedback from the participants and draw a conclusion, but this may not satisfy those providing the finances, who may be set on seeing numbers.

### 5. Can one do without a mentor?

Yes. Having a mentor is not essential to existence and progress. Many have treaded this path safely. However, there are many benefits to be had from having a mentor. But if one is satisfied and confident of making her/his own mark by herself/himself, one can do without a mentor too.

### 6. How do I find a mentor for myself?

Mentors don't announce themselves or advertise. If you are out to find a mentor for yourself, the best course would be to look for one in the higher echelons of your own organization or in your profession. Then the need would be to find out more about the person and broadly figure out your compatibility with the person before taking it forward. When satisfied, the person can be approached for consent and mutual exploration of expectations.

### 7. How do I know who is a suitable mentor for me?

If you need to assess the suitability of the mentor for you, a good idea would be to start with yourself. Find out more about yourself. Clarify what your expectations from mentoring are. What are your expectations from a mentor? How much are you investing in the process? When you have a fix on these, then you will have a good idea about who fits the bill. Please do remember that mentoring is a bilateral enterprise and it is not adequate to have a mentor who suits you. You also must suit the mentor.

### 8. How do I figure out the right kind of mentee for me?

To begin with, get a fix on the WIIFM (What's In It For Me). Then you will need clarity on the expectations you have from the mentee and what you can contribute to the mentee. This is half-way to the solution. The other half is rather unpredictable. Compatibility between two people and that too with a specific context to the relationship is extremely difficult to prescribe. But the best way to sort this out is to mutually explore compatibilities before venturing any further.

## 9. How do I build trust between the mentor/mentee and me?

There certainly is no quick-fix solution here. The 'well-known secret' in building trust is being trustworthy yourself. Besides, open communication and sharing helps the process along. Time is a good companion in this quest. You will have to do your part and then let time work the magic.

## 10. How do I enlist organizational support for the mentoring scheme?

There is a list of steps that can get you a buy-in from the organization for the mentoring scheme. The most important ones are: to target the right and strategic people in the top management team; get the right kind of people in the mentoring implementation team; give the scheme as much positive publicity as possible; get the message out about the benefits of the scheme to people in the organization; get people to enlist into the scheme; and finally, keep costs as low as possible without penny-pinching.

## 11. How do I ensure that the mentors are serious about mentoring?

Mentoring is not a job. Hence it is not something that one can force another to perform as demanded. For the seriousness to be inculcated in mentors in an organization-sponsored scheme, the best and perhaps the only way is to get the right kind of people on board. If you have got the wrong people in, you already are in trouble.

### 12. Can I enlist the help or assistance of others in the development of my mentee?

Most certainly yes. That is the big advantage of having a well-networked mentor. She/he can access resources better and provide the mentee with opportunities to interact and network more efficiently. It is not essential that you are the best in every field that the mentee and you are working on. Where you have access to better resources and people who can help the mentee, please do take the option freely.

### 13. Can the boss be a mentor?

There is much to be said on either side. The boss is best placed to study and understand the person as she/he works directly under her/him. Therefore the boss is the best person who can understand and devise the best developmental and growth plans for the person. Further, the boss is in a position to organize work to support such a plan. On the other hand, the boss also tends to be more task-focused and less development-focused. Also, there is the issue of comfort in the level of openness and how close one can get with the boss if she/he is also the mentor. Role conflicts can come up if the same person is the boss and the mentor. So, yes, the boss can be a mentor, but there are issues that need to be addressed.

### 14. Can the mentor be a person from another department?

Yes, the mentor can be a person from another department. But consider the advantages in having one from your own department first. For people starting off in their career or profession, it would be advantageous to have someone from their own department. In the early years, there is much to pick up about your own work and its nuances. At this time it would be advantageous to be mentored by someone from your own department. During this time, a mentor from another department would have to network with someone from your own department regarding the subtleties of your specialization. For people at later stages of their careers or professions, the department that the mentor belongs to does not matter so much. The other mentoring competencies and capabilities become more important as your own horizons widen.

## 15. Does the mentor have to be in the same profession?

Not necessarily. It would help if she/he is, but being from another profession is not a disqualification. The capabilities and the wisdom of the mentor and the capacity to look beyond the narrow confines of the profession are of importance. The mentor's sagacity in being able to visualize the prospects and recognize the potential in the mentee is what matters more.

## 16. What if the mentor infringes into the line manager's territory?

Ideally a situation like this should not arise. The mentor and the line manager are both concerned with the development of the mentee/subordinate, to maximize the realization of her/his potential and to turn her/him into a better person. While the line manager is likely to be more task-focused, the mentor is development-focused. The best way to resolve differences between the two would be for the two to engage in a dialog and work out how both can supplement each other. The mentor, being more sagacious and concerned with the welfare of the mentee, could take the lead in this matter. It will be good to have communication channels open and constantly used between the mentor and the line manager, for the good of the mentee and the success of the mentoring process.

## 17. What if the senior management is not convinced about the mentoring scheme?

In organizations, it is often very difficult to have schemes like this work when the senior management is not convinced about their efficacy. It is not a happy position to be in if the senior management is not convinced about the mentoring scheme. The best bet is to try and get them to come around. And if this is not possible, the step to be taken is to provide as much support as possible to the mentors without getting the senior management put off by this. By no means should the scheme be run surreptitiously. That is definitely dangerous and could boomerang on the leaders of the scheme. Also, expect lukewarm response from others too if the senior management is not with you.

## 18. Does a mentor have to be older than a mentee?

In the Indian environment, age does play a major role in commanding respect and having credibility. However, there is no set rule that the mentor has to be older than the mentee. What are important are the qualities, competencies and the skill of the mentor and her/his ability to carry the mentee with her/him.

## 19. Do mentors have to be teachers?

The nature of the mentoring activity encompasses teaching; but the mentor need not be a teacher. If helping a learner to learn is called a teaching activity, then mentors are teachers too.

## 20. Does having a mentor increase your chances of promotion?

If becoming better at the job and improving one's competencies and capabilities leads to promotion, then mentoring helps in that direction. However, it must be kept in mind that there is no direct link between mentoring and better chances of promotion in organizations.

## 21. Should you have only one mentor?

There certainly is no prescription that there can only be one mentor for each person. Multiple mentors are definitely a possibility, depending on the needs of the mentee and the willingness of the mentors. But care should be taken to keep them informed about the arrangement so as to head off any possibility of conflict and misunderstanding.

## 22. Is mentoring a complicated business?

There are certainly a lot of intricacies, hard work and detailing to be done in mentoring. Then again, working with people is in all likelihood a 'complicated business.' This is one of the reasons why seasoned and established professionals and wise people become mentors.

### 23. Should a mentor be chosen for you?

That is really your call. Both having one chosen for you and choosing one for yourself can work well if the relationship and the process go well. Compatibility is the primary issue here. If the person or system choosing the mentor for you knows you and the mentor well, it is good. Otherwise, you might as well take up the responsibility of choosing one for yourself.

### 24. Can mentors be trained?

What is important is the values and attitudes that people aspiring to become mentors have in the first place. If these are fine, then they can be trained to handle the process and imbibe skills to make a success of mentoring.

### 25. How long does a mentoring relationship last?

There is no time limit or restriction for the mentoring relationship. As long as the mentor can be of help to the mentee and there is a need for having the mentor, the mentoring relationship can go on. When these conditions no longer exist, then the relationship can still endure in a changed context, with the relationship no longer being as between a mentor and a mentee.

### 26. How confidential is the mentoring relationship?

The relationship and the transaction between the mentor and the mentee are to be considered extremely confidential. Only the two have access or are privy to the communication and the relationship. The involvement or intervention of a third person or party should ideally be only with mutual consent and prior knowledge. This protects the relationship and the mentoring process from being vitiated.

## 27. What if my mentee wants my advice on leaving the organization?

Now, this is a tough call and a dilemma. While the interest of the mentee is paramount for you as a mentor, there is also the commitment and loyalty to the organization to be considered. It will be a good idea to help the mentee evaluate the options that she/he has and give your opinion frankly, presenting both sides of the picture and also your concerns. Finally, it is important to leave it to the mentee to make the decision.

## 28. Does mentoring have to be one-on-one only?

Mentoring does not necessarily have to be one-on-one. There can be group mentoring too. In this the mentees are taken in a group and all of them have the advantage of access to the mentor. Here the issues and concerns of the people in the group may be similar and their options may also be similar. There is much to be gained in this, as there are different points of view and perspectives available to sharpen the decisions on the choices. The downside is that there is little or no customization of output from the process for the individual.

# suggested readings

Brounstein, M. 2000. *Coaching and Mentoring for Dummies*. Foster City, CA: IDG Books Worldwide.

Clutterbuck, D. 1998. *Learning Alliances: Tapping into Talent*. London: CIPD.

———. 2000. 'Ten Core Mentor Competencies', *Organisations and People*, 7, pp. 29–34.

———. 2001. *Everybody Needs a Mentor: Fostering Talent at Work*. London: CIPD.

Clutterbuck, D., and D. Megginson. 1999. *Mentoring for Executives and Directors*. Oxford: Butterworth-Heinemann.

Collins, A. 1979. 'Notes on Some Typologies of Managerial Development and the Role of Mentors in the Process of Adaptation of the Individual to the Organization', *Personnel Review*, 8, pp. 10–14.

Conway, C. 1998. *Strategies for Mentoring*. Chichester: John Wiley and Sons.

Gregg, C. 1999. 'Someone to Look Up To', *Journal of Accountancy*, 188, pp. 89–93.

Guptan, S.U. 1988. 'Paternalism in Indian Organisations', *ASCI Journal of Management*, 18(1), pp. 77–86.

Handy, C. 1993. *Understanding Organisations*. Harmondsworth: Penguin.

Ibarra, H. 2000. 'Making Partner: A Mentor's Guide to the Psychological Journey', *Harvard Business Review*, March–April, 78(2), pp. 146–55.

Jossi, F. 1997. 'Mentoring in Changing Times', *Training & Development*, 51(8), pp. 50–54.

Kizilos, P. 1990. 'Take My Mentor, Please!', *Training*, April, 27(4), pp. 49–54.

Klasen, N., and D. Clutterbuck. 2002. *Implementing Mentoring Schemes: A Practical Guide to Successful Programs*. Oxford: Butterworth-Heinemann.

Kram, K.E. 1983. 'Phases of the Mentoring Relationship', *Academy of Management Journal*, 26, pp. 608–25.

Lacey, M. 1999. *Making Mentoring Happen: A Simple and Effective Guide to Implementing a Successful Mentoring Programme*. Warriewood, NSW: Business and Professional Publishing Pty. Ltd.

Malderez, A., and C. Bodoczky. 1999. *Mentor Courses: A Resource Book for Trainer-Trainers*. Cambridge: Cambridge University Press.

Parsloe, E. 1992. *Coaching, Mentoring and Assessing: A Practical Guide to Developing Competence*. London: Kogan Page.

Parsloe, E., and M. Wray. 2000. *Coaching and Mentoring: Practical Methods to Improve Learning*. London: Kogan Page.

Virmani, B.R., and S.U. Guptan. 1991. *Indian Management*. New Delhi: Vision Books.

Whittaker, M., and A. Cartwright. 2000. *The Mentoring Manual*. Aldershot: Gower.

Wickman, F., and T. Sjodin. 1997. *Mentoring: The Most Obvious Yet Overlooked Key to Achieving More in Life than You Ever Dreamed Possible*. New York: McGraw-Hill.

Zachary, L.J. 2005. *Creating a Mentoring Culture: The Organization's Guide*. San Francisco: Jossey-Bass.

Zey, M. 1984. *The Mentor Connection*. Homewood, IL: Dow Jones–Irwin.

## Websites

www.andrewgibbons.co.uk
www.imeandyou.com
www.learningbuzz.com
www.mentorsforum.co.uk
www.mentoring-programs.com

# Index

# about the author

SUNIL UNNY GUPTAN heads Touching Lives, an organization working in the areas of life strategies, humanizing organizations, and emotional health. As founder of Touching Lives, he focuses on making a significant difference to the lives of people. His passion is in working with people and helping them help themselves.

Dr Guptan began his career as a journalist with the *Indian Express*, and later moved to Osmania University, Hyderabad, as a member of the faculty, to teach communication and journalism. From 1987 to 1997 he was Professor in the Human Resources Area at the Administrative Staff College of India (ASCI), Hyderabad. He moved to FORDE Consultants in mid-1997 as Director and, in mid-2006, left to devote his time to Touching Lives.

A popular consultant for the past two decades, Dr Guptan is associated with several organizations in India and abroad. As a leading trainer, he has advised chief ministers, cabinet ministers, top executives in industry and government, trade union leaders, and even schoolteachers in the areas of human relations and communication. He is also a Visiting Professor at the Indian Institute of Management, Ahmedabad. His work now focuses on individualized learning and development for senior executives through executive coaching and mentoring.

Based in Hyderabad, Dr. Guptan invests his personal time in counseling and helping people cope with and repair strained relationships and troubled lives. He also co-hosts, with his wife Surekha, a free Web portal on relationships, www.imeandyou.com.

You can contact Dr Guptan at mentor@touchinglives. co.in.